WHY DO SOME ENTREPRENEURS SUCCEED OR FAIL? **J. Rafael López**

WHY DO SOME ENTREPRENEURS SUCCEED OR FAIL? **J. Rafael López**

Classified as a scientific book and self-help for employers Intellectual Property Cadastre in Aragon (Spain) (RoyalDecree 1/1996, April 12. Legalization registered, April 27, 2003 CPR: 9053763, File - 2004e 0083281

JOSÉ RAFAEL LÓPEZ GÓMEZ
Author and owner of all rights.

ISBN 13: *978-1493769049*

ISBN 10: **1493769049**

WHY DO SOME ENTREPRENEURS SUCCEED OR FAIL? **J. Rafael López**

Sinopsys.

It is a manual to use for the entrepreneur who is not based on criteria "economic or financial theorists themselves." As its author, I wanted to share my long experience as an entrepreneur, paving the way to many people who have thought about creating your own business and financial independence, and not to engage not know how to start. The book includes a detailed listing of those things to keep in mind and frequent practical problems you may encounter the entrepreneur. It clearly explains the different performances of different businesses starting from planning development and operation, to the consumer. Recommended sectors, and all that is necessary to know not to fail in the attempt. <After a long and extensive experience in time, do not leave it to be an extremely useful guide more immediate today in these times of crisis, pointing out the future entrepreneur, that this, perhaps not just a vocation arises but of the need not to be tied to an unlikely gainful employment that can fail at any time This manual is intended for those people who, even without much preparation, can undertake activities as entrepreneurs who want to wean, and also to those other that having been entrepreneurs, have not found the success they sought.

José Rafael López Gómez-Spanish-After high school and before twenty, got the diploma in Industrial Master. The College of Industrial Engineering of Barcelona (EUETIB), and so it continues to identify. For a hundred years, the school has trained thousands of technicians known as experts, directors of industries, industrial technicians, industrial experts, technical engineers and finally industrial engineers. All have been active agents in the construction of the Catalonia we know today. (School Report University.)

THE BEST AND MOST EFFECTIVE WAY
TO CREATE, WORK AND BUSINESSES

Classified as a science book and self-help for employers
Have you thought about starting a business
or create your own work and do not know
or like to dedicate to start?
Here you will find what you want. We can help.

Manuals and help entrepreneurs start a
business as <Creación empleo>Entrepreneurs,
Companies, Planning, Assemblies, Facilities,
Manufacturing, Commercial, Sales,
Home Services, Construction,
Business Strategies, Secrets general>
<Hostelería in business.

INTRODUCTION 1-

The employment crisis! A possible consequence of economic development and of the excessive greed of all those people who don't act sensibly, looking at long-term benefits, with the lower classes with generally less money being those who are most negatively affected.

HAVE YOU THOUGHT ABOUT CREATING YOUR OWN BUSINESS BUT YOU DON'T KNOW WHAT TO DO OR EVEN WHERE TO BEGIN?

BARS, AND EVERYTHING RELATED TO THISSECTOR.

Learn how
to make different items for comercilaizarlos for wholesale bu sinessoutside catering, or mism0o time.
Some parefos following manual correspo0nden to "Succeed o r fail some enterprising" However, what you read about all the businesses that mean, you are going to assert throughout his life as EMPRTENDEDOR,

The solution is in your grasp within this book.
Dear readers, congratulations for choosing this book. You've just opened a window to the future, through which you will feel a cool breeze and that ray of sunshine that we all need sometimes. If this book found its way into your hands, it isn't just by chance. I know from personal experience that your head never stops telling you over and over again, **You have to do something with your life.** This book isn't a literary work or anything like it. Everything you read here is part of the experience of a long life setting up small businesses. Do you want to get lucky? Luck is an incredible miracle that we

all have from being born, and if we choose it, it can quite easily take us and drive us towards our goals. If you pay attention to what I suggest here, my experience gained over more than fifty years, luck will find you and will form part of what you carry with you, becoming your permanent companion.

The way I see it, luck is contagious and I'm going to try to transmit mine which was good to me. You'll find out how I managed to reach the end of my days without depending on others. I was free because I chose to be. With this message, you'll learn how to live your life independently forever. To be a WINNER, there are no tricks: all you need to do is **CHOOSE TO BE A WINNER**. If you really want it with all your heart, luck will follow you in every project you ever start. Success in any activity we do is intuition, feelings and enthusiasm, are what will make us **lucky** and decide how much we do.

Your dedication and my experience will be a perfect team to achieve whatever you choose. I can provide help, but without your collaboration, it won't be possible at all. My capacity for work was so great... that if they'd sold me the Giralda in monthly payments, I would have bought it, even if I didn't have the money. It was a way of seeing the world. I'm describing myself a little here so that you can take advantage of what I write and see businesses in the right way, as something easy to set up. Don't forget that you hold the key to unlocking wealth in your future: all you need to do is make the right decision. Well, let's get to work.

The best and most effective way to create work and Businesses .

Our aim is to fight the employment crisis, creating independent work, as well as small or large businesses. Some governments say that "All citizens have the right to a decent job" (which we agree with), but who creates those jobs? Who creates the work for so many unemployed? And that's where we come in. "The Entrepreneurs"

With this text and your participation, you will find the path to your own economic freedom, and there won't be anyone who can stop you. As such, you'll decide for yourself what you want to do with your life. Read this message to the end and today will have been "A Great Day for You".

What I explain in this manual is not "copies of other people's experience". They are the author's personal experiences of the various businesses he participated in during his long life as a businessman and entrepreneur.

If you've never worked before, you've finished studying, your business has closed due to the current crisis or you've been fired from the business you worked in, **REMEMBER THAT YOU'RE NOT ALONE!** My experience will become your future **SUCCESS.**

If you choose this path, **YOU, AND ONLY YOU, will be the PERSON IN CHARGE** of your own life who can achieve whatever you want, and as a consequence, you'll create work for yourself and others, finally discovering why businesses succeed or fail. You'll be able to avoid problems before they happen...

Before starting any business, you must take advantage of this advice and find out **WHAT BUSINESSMEN KNOW BUT DON'T TELL YOU.** After reading this, you'll know why your time working for others is wasted. Being an independent businessman starting from almost nothing is not so difficult. What's difficult is THE DESIRE, and in this text, you'll read everything you need to know to achieve it.

DO YOU KNOW ANY POOR BUSINESSMEN? Impossible! Poor businessmen DON'T exist. Do you want to know how to run a business and not fail, even if you've never done it before? Our experience is here for you to learn from. Take advantage of it.

Meet A REAL ENTREPRENEUR, find out what I learned through various jobs, during my entire life as a businessman, and learn how you can build an empire starting from nothing.

THE MENTAL CAPACITY TO REASON, PLAN, SOLVE PROBLEMS AND UNDERSTAND BUSINESS IDEAS IS SOMETHING WHICH IS LEARNED DURING WORKING AND STRUGGLING FOR YEARS.

You might say that you can also learn this by studying economy. That's true, but after studying, you have to put it into practice. And this is where you will learn those practical applications which any new entrepreneur needs, even if they haven't studied.

If you really want this, you can find happiness through work. After receiving this lesson in popular business economics, you'll have opened the window to a future through which a ray of happiness will come which is something we all need to some time. If you have no experience as a businessman and you want to try your luck with no advice, you're in charge of your actions and can do whatever you want.

Some people think "I'll set up a business to try". Many entrepreneurs have this attitude and fail because they don't take advantage of others' experience. You're unique in this world and no-one will stop you doing whatever you choose.

A small business owner doesn't necessarily need to have worked in a particular trade. The most important thing for success is to have real desire. Then I'll be there to make sure you don't fail. **Don't forget that YOU will move mountains in any popular business with this desire together with my experience.**

Congratulations for making it this far. When you finish reading this, you'll be ready to jump right into the business world, and you'll always remember what you read. If you fail because you didn't read carefully, it will be your own fault. If you ever have a doubt about this book, write to emprendedoresactivos@gmail.com and you'll receive an immediate response.

CHAPTER 1 - -3

BEGINNING AS A BUSINESS-PERSON 3

Creating a popular business is the topic of this 2nd part and, in particular, the catering business in general, both in the implementation and commissioning of some of these businesses, as well in the manufacture of certain well-described products for both retail and wholesale.

I recommend to future entrepreneurs that they apply themselves to my writings, which will help them to succeed at the first attempt at a business. It doesn't matter if you've never been in any trade union, since you'll find here everything you need to start working independently. Fifty years dedicated to different activities as a popular entrepreneur is enough time for me to talk with experience about luck, positive or negative effects, and the implementation of any large-scale retail activity.

You may have heard that no-one ever got rich by working. This is partially true. The important thing is to use our ideas, with the help of the ideas in this book and of other people to do the physical work, to get to where we want to be. True business sense is not making work for yourself. The important thing is to create your first business and let it grow as the work grows, so that our collaborators, when we have them, always have work to do. We mustn't forget that most entrepreneurs start alone, and then employ more staff when there is sufficient work to be done. You'll be surprised at what can be called luck, at how money is handled, and how a fortune can be earned through perseverance and dedication.

Throughout my writings, you'll get to know the way different activities work. You'll discover how easy it can be to start as an entrepreneur, how to start a business, modest though it may be, and how to securely go forward with the business until the end. Luck is the consequence of total dedication to what you do. In my first years of work, I discovered that it would never be possible for me to find a secure job which would give me enough money if I always depended on others. Some years later, when I stopped to think about and analyse my ideas at that time (people began to work as an apprentice at the age of 14 or 16 at that time), I worked out that I didn't want to join the working world forever. From a young age,

I always had the idea of doing something big which would rid me of any debts and mediocrity. At first, I did a few little jobs on my own until I started working as an apprentice. I soon discovered that working for someone else, I would never realise my dream and would never be proud of what I did. Well, I was a shy boy, a consequence of my needs and lack of money, a municipal school and not much else. I remember when I was around twelve years old, one day, I went to the cinema to see the film

"Snow White and the Seven Dwarves". I bought a ticket and was near the front of the queue to get a good seat. There were so many parents with their children that the tickets for that section sold out quickly. I was waiting for them to open the door so I could go running to the top floor: the cinema had various floors and the seats were wooden benches. At that moment when I was waiting, I heard a shout amid all the excitement which said "Who will sell their ticket?!" Nobody answered, and a little later I heard it say, "I'll pay double what it's worth!", my heart skipped a beat and without thinking, I answered "I'll sell it!" The ticket cost two pesetas and I sold it for four. I felt so excited when I realised that I could earn money without even being a man yet. I kept on making money with this business while the film ran. I was very careful that my parents didn't find out in case they gave me a good beating for doing something that didn't seem right to them. Afterwards, I was watching the films that they put on at the weekends.

My job consisted of going to school and then "working" on Saturdays and Sundays. When I was fourteen, I started making pasta which I sold in food shops... which I talk about in the 1st part, "for entrepreneurs". Despite my young age, I realised that if you don't have a degree or a well-paid job, it's much harder for you to earn a living. I thought, if I work for others during my whole working life, will I be able to have the things rich people have? Will my salary be good enough that I'll never need for anything at the age I need it most? My worst nightmare was having to work my whole life as a wage-earner. Just thinking about it made me feel terrible, as if someone was burning me from the inside! My idea at that time was to start on a different path. I understood that it wasn't possible if I didn't stop working for myself as soon as possible. Thoughts raged through my mind and wouldn't stop. What if I went to the Americas? At that time, many people emigrated to South America. And I, as a dreamer of impossible dreams, was happy to go to the port in Barcelona and see ships laden with travellers rom other countries. Those ships held so many hopes! But... here we are. I discovered that to earn money, it isn't necessary to go to another country nor to work as an employee. I found that with any job I did on my own, I earned as e much money in ten days as I did in a month working as an employee.

Without thinking about it too much, I decided to work for myself. These personal explanations will justify the truth of my experience of so many years. These days, people talk about unsecure retirement pensions after having paid social security during an entire life as an employee. What kind of pension does a person who works for someone else all their life have at the end, when a secure economic situation is most needed? When you grow older, after having worked as an employee all your life, what pension are you left with? Your income might not be enough but you have to put up with it. So what can you do if your income is enough to save a little in order to guarantee well-being in life when you most need it? If you stop and think about it, as I did, your brain will tell you who you should work for for the rest of your working life.

WORKING FOR YOURSELF OR FOR OTHERS. 4

Even if you have been focused on finding a secure job in someone else's business, maybe after reading this, you'll change your way of thinking and become a future entrepreneur. If you don't have the money to start a modest business, this book will give you formulas to start from very little, or even from nothing. If the idea of being an entrepreneur doesn't interest you, what you read here will help you become a model employee, indispensable to the company you work for. You'll find that businesses depend on you. But clearly I don't want you to learn from my experience for the benefit of your boss.

When we have the desire to be successful and conquer, success will be with us wherever we are, whether we work as employees or entrepreneurs. Doing what you're doing is thinking about only what you do. You already know what awaits you if you decide to be an employee, that you could be a good worker in someone else's company, with no more hope than retiring and, as a reward, getting a decent pension.

On the other hand, you could take an entrepreneurial role and you'll always have this book at your disposal when you need it. My anecdotes and advice here are the product of my experience, so don't let them go to waste because you never know when you'll need them. Any job or business is a battle which must be won ahead of time using forethought, before committing to them. I started at the age of fourteen, doing anything to make money. The few resources I had did nothing to take away my dream. But the desire to do something different was so strong that it led me to accept that struggle that I had proposed to myself. I'm sure that if you can take advantage of my experience, you'll prove to yourself that you're intelligent, with enough important data that you won't fail.

ALWAYS FORWARDS. 5

Your freedom begins when you create your own company, be it big or small. The beginning of a modest business could be the best solution as to the first step to take. I always talk about the situation a new, inexperienced entrepreneur finds themselves in. A young child needs to be taken by the hand when taking their first steps until they are able to walk alone. In businesses, the same thing happens. When you learn a trade, any business is completed as if it were a game. Once I heard someone say: "I started a company and I started to live." Don't pay much attention to those stories without foundations since, when you begin your first company, you'll have responsibilities you never even considered.

That's a tribute to your independence. Are you thinking that I'm taking a long time in talking about specific companies? The idea of the project found in this book is that before talking about having your own company, I want you to know in advance why an entrepreneur fails or succeeds.

In this book, you'll find instructions for how to begin from nothing. With your first business, you'll start to realise your dreams, as long as you have a lot of willpower. Starting a business is like learning to drive. When you have a licence you can already drive. After a little time, you can take other people with you and be the best driver there is. In the same way, practice is what you need to be a good business person. After a little time, you'll understand how practically any business works.

If you don't want to make your brain work too much, the easiest thing is to start a franchise of an existing product. In this case, what you do would depend on the rules and regulations of others. As a franchising entrepreneur, you would have to pay a kind of entry fee (an amount of money in order to be able to sell the product and use its name in promotions and adverts for your business). You would pay a certain percentage of all sales, and another percentage for publicity.

And you would need the necessary capital to get a building and get it up to the franchiser's standards. You would need to buy the product from them, or whatever other arrangement you come to. Any future entrepreneur can learn a lot by visiting franchising exhibitions as samples. Later, I'll talk about how this works exactly. If you're interested in franchises, go to the Chamber of Commerce in any major city where they will give you information.

In Spain, you can search in the Barcelona telephone directory, or on the Internet: "División de Franquicias" ("Franchising Division") or "Tormo & Asociados", which is a company which manages many franchises. Ah, but don't think that starting a business of whatever, with or without a franchise, will be enough, because if we don't do everything in our power in terms of ambition, effort and willpower, we won't get a thing.

WORKING AS AN EMPLOYEE AND HAVING NO RESPONSIBILITIES. 6

There are many people whose livelihoods depend on a job. The difference is that if you work for someone else, you go when they tell you to, and when you work for yourself, you go to work knowing that you'll find some new adventure every day and a new challenge, and this eagerness will help fuel your own Economic Freedom I became independent by creating my own small business from which others emerged. At the end of my long working life, which lasted close to fifty years, I asked myself: Why shouldn't I help other people to make their dreams come true? People who work their entire lives as employees in others' companies only to end up with empty pockets? Many books are written for entrepreneurs which speak about percentages, sales per year and per sector, which make large-scale economic calculations, forgetting that not all new entrepreneurs have huge budgets to begin with, and not understanding the juggling acts people have to perform in financial engineering. They never tell you that, to be good, the coffee you drink in a bar only weighs ten grams. That's the difference between buying this book and others. With my writings, you'll discover ways of negotiating to make money and what to do so that any job you do, regardless of how humble it may be, will be finished successfully.

INGENUITY HELPS US. 7

Eating too much dulls your senses. Let's be sensible, get up from dinner still a little bit hungry and our ingenuity will rise to the surface. The largest worry for great inventors and discoverers is developing their ideas and drawing up a plan, a business idea or the development of a future invention. When a business project is planned, the biggest worry is that it works well and that the profits come as a consequence. However, those people that don't think and don't innovate to change their lives are also very important for society. They are the best collaborators for development in any country, for their participation in work and buying and selling your products. If you have come up with an idea, give it your full attention and patience and you'll find a way to make it possible. The business ideas that I talk about here, though some will have nothing to do with your projects or trade, will help you t discover new horizons, and may serve as a template which you can use to develop your own ideas. This book is mostly aimed at new entrepreneurs in general, and at those that started a new business which didn't work out. If this book falls into the hands of a professional, there will be chapters which mention businesses they may have heard of, and to learn from others' mistakes.

DOWHATEVER YOU'REDOING 8

Any future entrepreneur doesn't waste time on trivial matters. They are ambitious by nature and always want something more than the great majority of other people. They aren't satisfied with traditional jobs or trades. They demand self-improvement every day. As an entrepreneur, they put all their energy into the job that they are doing now, and then the next one, and so on. When an artist paints a picture, they are immersed in their work and, for them, the world around them doesn't exist. They feel as if they are floating in space, transported to another dimension. They are completely immersed, and finally they complete their masterpiece. The entrepreneur that immerses himself in his work will always reap the benefits. When I was between thirty-five and forty, besides my own businesses, I studied in my spare time in the Zaragoza Art School, and afterwards, went to study painting in a painting studio called Cañada. When I was painting, it was as if nothing existed outside of the canvas I was painting. In that moment, I didn't even remember about my business. I only thought about what I was doing. And when I finished the class, I went back to my work. At that moment in my life,

I only did what I was doing at that moment.

Entrepreneurs have to act with true enthusiasm and dedication and, in any job or business that they start, they have to try to improve every day. At the beginning, they'll make small businesses and make a little money until they think of a brilliant idea one day. Mind you, when I was young, writing with wooden pencils or metallic pens which had to be dipped in ink in an old, hard inkwell on the school desk. Something which others had already invented before. Then came the fountain pen. And now, we usually write with a ballpoint pen. This was the idea of a Hungarian journalist, László Bíró. He had problems with the fountain pen when he wrote, and sometimes the ink stained his pockets.

He started thinking about how to solve the problem, when at last it came to him. He found that a small ball fitted onto the end of a small cylinder would roll on the paper, resulting in a line of ink. He patented it in 1938 in his home country, Hungary. He later emigrated to Argentina, where he worked on the project for five or six years until he perfected it. Later he sold the patent in different countries. Today, they are sold around the entire world. It's an example of the great wealth we all have in "our heads".

BEING WIDE AWAKE WHEN YOU'RE NOT ASLEEP. 9

Future entrepreneurs must be awake at any moment and their brains have to act as a constantly-moving radar, analysing everything the eyes see and ears hear. Being a silent observer, ideas will come all at once, being analysed one after the other, and saving any which seem to have a future for use whenever needed. Of course, some of my ideas won't be used due to economic reasons, but only some of them.

Freedom and luck don't choose you, you choose them. If you

working situation up to now has been working in other companies, and now you want to enter into the world of the entrepreneurs, you have to realise that it is a work of independent fighters. Freedom and independence are bought with sacrifice and effort. At the beginning of your life as an entrepreneur, you won't have fixed working hours. Your business will decide that according to its needs...When you get up in the morning, give yourself a shower, ending it with cold water, and if one day you don't have time, put your head under the tap, get the back of your neck wet, and you'll see that the cloud in your eyes that you have when you wake up disappears. Entrepreneurs, from waking up to going to bed must be alert, quick and intuitive. As you get used to running a business, you'll get closer to any objective in your reach. In the American west, any person who didn't lacked those reflexes and ability to anticipate would die. In the world of business, any time someone goes to market would a different product, a new idea, a different way of running a business, or opening a business in a good location, it is a consequence of their reflexes and imagination. We're not talking about competition here. There are competitors here with a new product, a good chance of being successful. Luck is on their side. It all depends on your instinct and how awake you are when you take action.

INITIAL CAPITAL. 10

I once heard someone say that the most difficult part is earning your first million pesetas. Work and economy taken forward with security can make miracles, and you can achieve what many others have achieved throughout the years. Every era has its opportunities, and we all have moments in our lives when things go better than other times. When we find luck is on our side, we don't let it get away. We continue taking advantage of it. Really though, what they call luck is actually just the reward for our hard work and ingenuity. I remember that in an ice-cream business, the iced drinks we served were so cold, the sales were continuous.

Work started with breakfast at five in the morning, and continued the entire day - in summer - with the manufacture and sales of ice-creams and iced drinks. We didn't take breaks or holidays for quite a long time. My wife and I were tired and decided to sell the business. We got lucky, or maybe it was a result of thinking like a customer. When you start a new business project, think about what the customers want and what you want yourself, and you'll have a good source of ideas.

You can find more about the manufacture of those ice-creams and those very special iced drinks in more of my writings. Money attracts money. If it is saved and invested, more and more will be earned, because if it is spent as it is earned, one will never have the economic power necessary to build a larger business. With what you save, together with a loan, you can start your first business. But, if you've got nothing, you're not alone. You still have yourself which is still a lot. In one of the paragraphs in this chapter, you'll read about "extra jobs", which can help you earn the money you need to start as from nothing.

GET USED TO THINKING. 11

Don't tell anyone that you spend time just thinking. Those that don't think will think you're not normal. They don't know the amount of people that their time thinking about businesses and about how to set themselves up to attract compulsive customers, creating an infinite range of products and services which makes them happy. When one better understands a certain product, the customers themselves, the sector or the market in which you want to enter, you're more certain of success. If you talk about business matters with your family or friends, it'll be a waste of time. If you tell them you'll work more because you want to save, they'll ask you the old question: "What for? You already earn enough to live...". If you tell them you want to become independent, they'll think you're escaping from a gang or other group. If you're not strong in your ways, they'll change your mind which could be what is most convenient for them. Be cautious and don't say anything person about your projects.

BRAND MARKET, WEAKER ECONOMY   12

Don't even think about brand products or articles. They are usually more expensive than everyday brands. The cheaper ones fulfil the same purposes. "Please, give me the best shoes you have. I'm poor," said a man politely when buying some shoes in a shop that I used to run. Those words disconcerted the shop assistant. The customer said to her: "Miss, don't be confused. I can't buy myself shoes every six months. I need some which will last me two years." Sensible economy. The first objective you have to consider is to intelligently value your time and money before spending it. Buy where the best price and best quality products are, in either large or specialist markets. You have to budget without leaving yourself short for what you need. Spending money on luxuries, which make up the majority of things that surround us in our homes, you can ensure that you never save any money. It's a stage which you have to go through with discipline and humility, and it's not so difficult that you'll never make it. We have to act as a kind of dictator, never spending anything which isn't necessary.People often say "Without money, you can do nothing", and to that, we can add "and without willpower to achieve an objective, it'll be less than nothing". It's more difficult every day to start a business if you don't have enough money. When we don't have it, thoughts go round and round in our heads.

Who can lend me some? If money was so easy to get, just with a pat on the back, nobody would work and nothing would ever be created. When you have some property and guaranteed invested money, financial institutions or banks will lend it to you.

Those properties are placed at the mercy of these lenders under a contract which states that, if you can't pay back the money, you run the risk of losing the property. They'll auction it off and take the money for the debt. If you're a worker and good with money, something you don't have to tell people who already know you, they know if they can trust you, and if they can lend you their savings, but if they don't have any, they can't do anything to help you. And if they had them, they'd think twice before lending them. In summary, you're alone, and it has to be you, with your intelligence and willpower, who finds the formula to make a little money and start off that business which, in time, will bring you more. A mouse can eat a whole wheel of cheese with patience, eating piece by piece until they finish. Starting from little, with a small business, you can get to wherever you want, but only by being ambitious, balanced and active.

MY PROPOSAL, IF YOU HAVE NOTHING. 13

With the jobs that I'll propose to you, you won't have much free time but, if you have any, go to a library and you'll find many books that you'll need. Become a member of one of them and you can take the ones you need home to start studying those business ideas you've got in your head. There are books of all types: sales, manufacture, plumbing, looking after birds, catering, being a waiter, IT. Whatever you have in your head can be filled out with a good book. You can also do a course on whatever subject is most convenient.

Other people have worked and written for people like me or you, and the only way to thank them and take advantage of them is by reading them. From now on, your fate is in your hands (and your future defined by only you), so you can choose to do whatever you want. You can choose one path, the one leading to a better economic situation or be poor your whole life. Of course, we can't know how long we'll live exactly, but meanwhile we can try to live better and have more excitement. Or we can work to live and die with empty pockets. They are the options to choose. Time is money, which sounds good, but this is your time and the only rea fortune you have available which you must take advantage of. Forget about TV, the thief in your house, a pastime which you must do without. The word "pastime" is clear itself, meaning "pass time without creating or producing", and you aren't the kind of person to waste your time, isn't that right? That is, apart from the news, because it's not bad to be well-informed. To future entrepreneurs, the ones that worry me, I say you have to control your time because it's very easy to lose it. Time wasted is money wasted. Well, at my age, things change. I watch TV more than I should and do other things like reading and painting. The battleground belongs to you. There is money to be earned. It's your turn. Other people are willing to spend.

EXTRA JOBS, A GOOD SOURCE OF INCOME.14

Important. Here is an idea so you can start from nothing. You'll have to work in another company on the weekends you have available. I'm assuming here that you have absolutely nothing, not even a trade.

Does that seem OK? Well, most people who read this book will, I suppose, have enough culture and knowledge. Even so, there are some who have fewer opportunities than others.

Living in this world is a form of "luck" for young people, another type of luck where we older people would have loved to have lived. If we didn't need to work to live, there'd be a long queue to sign up for that, but unfortunately it's not as easy as that. The truth is different, and even though they now pay for studying, you have to work to live. Maybe you don't have any money, dear reader, but you do have enough knowledge to understand my message. My writings are so popular because they have as much value to people who know a lot as to those who don't. Living in this world is a form of "luck" for young people, another type of luck where we older people would have loved to have lived. If we didn't need to work to live, there'd be a long queue to sign up for that, but unfortunately it's not as easy as that. The truth is different, and even though they now pay for studying, you have to work to live.

 Maybe you don't have any money, dear reader, but you do have enough knowledge to understand my message. My writings are so popular because they have as much value to people who know a lot as to those who don't.

Let's suppose that you work in a company during the week but not the weekends, because, otherwise, you're "trapped", my good friend. You have to arrange something so that you have those days free and to have them available to do what you want. If that's impossible, change your job. Maybe you're a waiter or any other job which works at weekends. If that's the case, leave your job and look for one which doesn't work at weekends.

That leaves you with eight days a month to spend in another job which could be a waiter. It's funny, isn't it? The other job that you do on the weekdays, whether it be in an office, a workshop, as a labourer, a night watchman, a policeman or whatever else, the important thing is that you be available at the weekends so that you can work extra and double your monthly salary. You'd like to, wouldn't you? OK, let's get to work.

WORKING AT WEEKENDS. 15

Catering businesses work more at the weekends than on other days and need extra staff on Saturdays, Sundays and all holidays. Let's give an example: cafés and restaurants which don't close any day of the week need to have more staff than normal so that they can have at least one or two to cover every day. They always depend on having so many staff but, even so, many businesses of this type need extra staff to work on weekends. That's where you come in. You can offer to work those days, regardless of the hours, as long as they pay you. Even better, they usually give you your meals for free in those places.

Your offer has to be to work the entire weekend and not just a few hours which are convenient for them. At the beginning, you can do any kind of work in a business of this type, helping the waiters, in the kitchen or whatever suits the company, which will all help your objective. If you've never worked as a waiter, you'll quickly learn that it's essential to get by. You'll learn by practice. If you get a job which doesn't suit you, keep trying different ones until you find a good one, and not just whatever suits the company. You'll get a job for an afternoon, not for life. You caccept them for now while it suits you to practice, but don't stop looking. If you get stuck in that one-afternoon job and don't keep looking, you're doing it wrong.

FAST-FOOD COMPANIES. 16

If you're not qualified enough, let me give you some advice. The most important thing, apart from the exposure, is a waiter's dynamism. People who don't move around very much in their jobs have no future. If you are the one who has to charge the customers in one of these café or other businesses, remember that the boss or manager of the business knows a lot about money matters. A thief who wants to take what isn't theirs won't last long in a job like this. Do your job with honour and don't look around when they're paying you to see if you're being watched. If you act as you should, without a doubt you'll keep your job as long as you want it. Restaurant owners have been around the block a few times and, as clever as a member of staff is, they are more so. The biggest and best-known fast-food restaurants are good for students because they are open every day, even bank holidays. They can also be a good source of extra work when it suits you. You won't make as much as in other restaurants, but the important thing is to work at the weekends.

Have a good look at how every job you do is completed. It might serve you well when you open your own first company. If you offer to work as a waiter or bartender, and you've never done it before, you can tell them you're not a professional but that you can get by, since you helped out at a friend's or relative's bar, etc. These half-truths won't be very important but will give you a hand at first. When a catering business needs staff and can't find any professionals, they'll take what they can. Working as a waiter or bartender on busy days makes you learn quickly.

Try watching them while they do their job. If you want to learn something else, you can find books on the catering industry in any public library, with which you can learn how to set a table, put the cutlery correctly, on which side to serve a customer and take away the plates, some of the more common cocktails, and the number of some of the common things in catering.Reading a book on catering can help you look good in front of your professional colleagues by learning enough to work with those services. After a while, it will

become a routine, like working in a factory. Many figures of modern history worked a waiter when they began working. This type
of work can be found in any country or place in the world.

SEARCHING FOR MORE INTERESTING WORK 17

In every major city, there are restaurants that serve banquets at weekends and pay extra to their employees to work them. The services generally begin with dinner on Friday night and finish on the Sunday evening. If you don't know the trade or how to be a waiter, offer to work doing whatever they need, watching everything, taking mental notes of everything you see, and soon you'll know how to be a waiter. Once you're working at one of these companies, you'll discover how easy it is by watching the waiters. You'll learn quickly and pretty soon you'll be one of them. Being a good professional waiter is one thing and learning the basics in order to get by is another, which is what I'm proposing to you.

When you go along to ask for work in the catering trade, in a restaurant or café with vacancies, dress very smartly and be polite when greeting anyone you meet. This job requires this behaviour, otherwise doors will be shut in your face. Ask for the manager, owner or chief of personnel, depending on the class and size of the company. When you tell them about your wish to work at weekends, make them feel good by telling them about how important you think the company is according to its values. This will be the perfect moment to start speaking. Look into the eyes of the person you're talking to. Start by telling them you have a regular job with insurance and that you are currently available at weekends.

This businessman wants to hear from your lips that you have a job and insurance (even if you don't, or if it's a half-truth), that you like working in catering, and that your nature is to always be doing something. It's not a bad idea to praise yourself occasionally at times as good as this. Be modest,

You need support to ensure you don't fall.graceful, and don't be shy with people that receive you. This will help you get their attention. It's a question of winning over the person you're talking to.
Don't tell these businessmen and managers about your needs because they want to employ people without problems. If they ask you why you want to work more, since you already have a job, tell them you want to save for the future. Remember that they're watching you at this time. If they offer you a drink, refuse or, at most, ask for tap water which they shouldn't mind. If they tell you that they don't need any more staff at the moment, leave them a business card for them to call you back. You've now given them a good impression of your positive personality and your telephone number. In these businesses, waiters work with the public and the manager or owner wants them to be smart and polite. For a catering manager, where food is handled, personal cleanliness is essential at all times, not just at first sight. Dazzle them with a good presentation and, if they need a member of staff, the job will be yours. If they accept you, ask how much they pay per service or per hour, without insisting too much on a good salary, since they'll pay you the same as everyone else there. In this case, the hours of working at banquets start with setting the tables and serving the food, and finishes with the desserts and coffees.

ANOTHER OF FINDING THESE JOBS.   18

Ask waiters at restaurants or major cafés to find extra work at weekends and, if they don't know, ask another, as many as necessary.   One of them will know. In this trade, communication is very important. Many people have a good job and work at weekends as a waiter in a café or large restaurants. If you've learned enough to work as a waiter and they ask you to work at a banquet, don't worry. Put on some good trousers, black shoes, a white shirt, or ask or have a look at the clothes the other waiters wear. Ask your colleagues if they wear a jacket or a waistcoat, and if they wear a special colour. The traditional colour is black. If there is a specific uniform, the company will provide that. If the clothing is traditional, they should direct you to buy them in a special shop. They'll give you the direction when the job is yours. Practice carrying two or three plates in one hand, or several glasses full of water and a bottle on a tray. It will be good practice for your balance to get you used to the job. Try carrying two plates of cold food, no soup, in your left hand, and in your right, whatever you can safely put on the table.

I'll tell you something that happened to me as a youngster working as a waiter. In banquets, there are various plates of hors d'oeuvres and fried food which the waiters serve directly from the tray they hold in one hand, while they use the other hand to serve the food to the customer using tongs. They use a fork and a spoon as tongs, held in one hand and used with skill.

Many waiters take pride in being able to do this very well. When I found it I had to do that but still hadn't worked out how, I found a shop and bought some small tongs used in bakeries, just really a piece of folded stainless steel. When the time came that I had to serve the hors d'oeuvres, took the tongs from my pocket and served them as well as anyone else. I forgot about professional pride without even intending to. I felt a little silly but acquitted myself quite well. What I'm saying here is that you mustn't "make a mountain out of a molehill". Everything can be solved with time, just by thinking.

Planning ahead of time gives good results. My plan was to buy the tongs. I never imagined that some years later, I would have about fifteen waiters as employees in my restaurant. If you've never worked as a waiter in a banquet before, you might be wondering how much you can earn in a weekend. In 2004 in Zaragoza, they were paying over 90 euros for each service. Four weeks multiplied by four services each week, multiplied by 90 euros makes 1,440 euros. I don't mean that every place would pay you this. Some will be more and others less. But on average, it's a pretty good salary. The difference is that this job is done while other people are having a good time. What can we say about this? That they enjoy the party while others are making their fortune. Every time I revise this book, the salaries and prices are rising.

WHAT YOU CAN EARN AS A WAITER - IN BANQUETS. 19

The money that can be made in this way in four weekends is as much as working for a month in a normal job. I'll give you an example: in 2004, an office assistant or a shop assistant could make, including insurance, between €800 and 900 a month, more or less. Imagine that in one weekend there are four banquets: Friday night, Saturday midday and night, and Sunday midday. Four banquets by four weeks would mean that there are 16 banquets per month. The hours you'll work at a banquet could be from an hour before the banquet until the tables used are cleared. You begin by setting the tables and, if you eat at the company, which is often free and before the service starts, you'll arrive a little earlier. Imagine that there are only 10 banquets a month at 90 euros per service. That would make around €900. It's clear that companies that run this kind of service are usually busy every weekend for pretty much the entire year. Here, I'm always talking about large cities with a large population.

RESTAURANTS THAT SPECIALISE IN BANQUETS 20

Don't forget that what these companies need are formal, dynamic, reliable people. Make sure you go to work, no matter what. The only viable excuse here would be that you've been run over by a lorry or that you're dead! OK, well, that's just a joke, but let's try to think in that way when we work.

In catering in general, there are only a few hours available to try to get as much money as possible, so in that time, you have to work as fast as possible in order to take advantage of that time. In the catering trade, there is a very good opportunity for working and studying. In summer resorts, they always need employees and some even provide accommodation. If you want to study but you don't have the means to do so, it's just a question of getting a job like this. From finishing your studies to starting, offer to work double shifts and you'll earn more without having to work during your study time. Even so, if the aim is what we've been talking about, you can even work weekends while studying and, if you can get work during the holidays, you can get extra money then. In this way, you can work and study the degree you want. Many have done this before and many others will do so in the future.

WORKING EXTRA TO INCREASE YOUR INCOME. 21

If you currently have a standard job, these extra jobs can help you reach the first rung on the ladder. Doing extra jobs is not a new invention. It has always existe and it will always exist, wherever you are. Let's say that you work from Monday to Friday and you live with your parents or in a rented apartment. If you don't have anything, it's a luxury living in an apartment for the amount of money that you have to spend. By buying the bare minimum, you can spend half of your money on necessities and save the other half. But let's not fool ourselves here. You might have nothing, but you've still got yourself which is worth quite a lot more than nothing. Remember that you are unique. From now on, your brain will be your slave driver and your body is your slave. They only want you to work hard and spend little. It's not a very good idea, is it? But if you're willing to get to where you want to be starting from nothing, it has to be like this. Otherwise, you'll continue as you are now and never get anywhere...Raw materials in industry are the unused or processed materials or components which businesses use to create their products.

You are the vital raw material needed to create your own world and means of living until you achieve your objectives. Remember that you're the most important person in the universe and, if you want, you can reach the goals you're proposing. First comes sacrifice and later abundance, and you only need to tighten your belt until you get there.

Don't think that you'll be the first or the last to live in this way, spending little, working many hours every day and saving a little money. You know what they say, that if you want something, you have to pay for it, and if it's worth it, you'll have to juggle what you earn so that your savings grow. One thing is clear. With these new jobs that I'm proposing, you won't just earn money; you'll also understand more about businesses and how they work, which will help you find the business you want.

You should live a frugal life, spending as little as possible, regardless of how much money you're earning. When you miss being outside, you have to be strong. The weak will end up drinking in a bar and the strong will learn where the public water fountains are and drink for free. With willpower, you can live for a day in summer without drinking and nothing bad will happen. That's where the strength of the conquistadors came from, having an iron will.

MAY YOUR IDEAS PREVAIL. 22

When it comes to planning a business, take advantage of your family's and friends' ideas because, for them, some may be useful to you but not to them. Sometimes, the ideas or experience of others can be vital in completing an objective. Listen well, speak little. Listen to others' opinions about work, businesses and everything that could be of interest.

Then you can consider and compare these ideas and do whatever it most convenient for you. Don't take action without forward planning. Any business can fail due to taking action before considering its implications.
No matter how much I say on the subject of businesses, it will never be enough. There are various economic newspapers and magazines in which you can read how large companies merge. How takeovers are completed. They buy other companies with money loaned to them by banks. They almost never pay with cash. When it comes to large, important companies, they gather money loaned from various banks with the companies' guarantee. This is a clear example that banks lend money to those who already have properties.
 These companies get loans to buy or start up new businesses. If these businesses paid in cash, it would cost them quite a lot more, since the money would come from the profits earned by others who would have to be a huge amount of tax once the tax returns are completed, almost as much as the money that would be paid to buy the new company. You might say, what does that matter to me? It's good to know about as much as possible, and if you already know it, even better for you. It's very lucky to have information about anything, since your

knowledge could be vital at any moment. It's the way it works: I set up a business with the money they loan me and then pay it off with the money I make from that business. The cost of the loans is discounted because of any credits owed and recovered, and the business ends up paying almost nothing. Well, these are just short explanations. An expert would explain it to you much better than I could. My explanation may not be perfectly correct since I'm only saying what I think but it's pretty close to the truth. If you want to grow and make a fortune, you clearly have to do it with loans, since waiting until you have enough money to create a large business will take you a long time to achieve.

I remember refurbishing one of the branches of my business (which I ended up renting out). I paid for this refurbishment in cash. (With a legal invoice of course.) In my tax return, I deducted ten percent each year of the cost of the invoice until it was paid off. As you can see, the refurbishment was deducted from the profits that I had to pay the state. I feel like the refurbishment was free for me. Laws often change so right now, your lawyer will know better that me what you should do.

When you start a business, as small as it might be, success depends on the attention you pay to it. Don't be happy with your business growing and progressing in slow-motion. You have to research, using everything you can, the best way to produce and sell your product or service better, driving out all competition if necessary. Don't set your prices the same as your nearest neighbours.

Always sell at a lower price and the best possible quality. Your business is just starting, while your nearest competitors may have been around with some time with all their loans paid off or maybe they are unambitious. You have to be inventive; you're going to war in order to win. It may be that your business is located in an area with many customers and little competition. If that's the case, you've hit the jackpot. You'll be able to sell at good prices, as long as it lasts. I'm talking about competition, but if you're in a place with little public demand, being inventive is pointless. When it comes to starting a business which sells directly to the public, your priority has to be a location where many people walk in front of your establishment. The location and the type of business you have always have to be related.

STARTING A BUSINESS 23

When you start your first competitive business, your sales will go up. You might earn less for each thing you sell, but at the end of the day, your profit will have increased. The logic of selling cheap is very simple: if you sell 100 with a 30% profit, you know that you will earn 30. But if you sell 300 in the same time period with a 25% profit, or even less, you'll sell cheaper but your profits overall will be much higher. You can be sure that selling at a high price won't get you far, while selling at a low price will cause your prices to go up every day. Everything is related to the type of business and your chances of doing it one way or another.

Some people don't like lowering their prices too much because they are desperate to make friends with their neighbours or other people in the same trade. These people are not competitive for various reasons. They are afraid or lazy, happy with what they have, or they weren't the ones who earned the money to make the business. Competitive entrepreneurs will also succeed at whatever they decide to do, leaving their mark wherever they go. The others will never be remembered.

I did all my activities as an entrepreneur in certain areas of Barcelona and Zaragoza (Spain), which are cities with large populations, where competition is real and businesses are achievable. In other villages, without having enough people, there is little demand and the competition is not very generous. The best place to fight these battles with other businesses is in the most populous areas of cities with large amounts of consumers.

WHAT IS BEHIND WHAT CONSUME?   24

Behind everything we consume, there are suppliers, composed of small and medium businesses and large consolidated companies, and in every one of these, there are people whose job is to think. Their brains never rest. They're always looking for ways to generate work for the company, create or discover new products at lower prices. In spite of all this, every day, businesses close and new ones come along. Some because the owner retires, others because of bankruptcy or because they were short-term businesses. Others because they weren't able to make the business fit with reality or the changing times, and others because their location wasn't chosen well. New companies are created with such preparation and desire that they devastate the whole battleground and others without any great aspirations. They die according to how they are born. Some businessmen began by manufacturing a few articles or creating services by having studied in advance where and who would be their best customers and if there would be enough demand to achieve enough sales. Sometimes small or large failures are brought about because they don't have the experience or advice from trustworthy people.

These days, you can't simply start a business to live from it. You have to move forward as soon as you commit to any activity because, as I said before, companies die according to how they are born. When a business is opened, sales are usually slow until customers start coming. Many entrepreneurs, upon seeing that they aren't making enough to cover costs, become desperate and leave the company, suffering the consequences. If we had a magic wand saying "This business will work and earn money from day one", it would be marvellous.

On the other hand, the general expenses in a business may be the same working a lot or working little. When we talk about working a lot in businesses, we mean selling a lot. To begin with, don't limit the articles you offer or the amount of hours you work. An entrepreneur can choose whether to work a lot and succeed or work little, live a comfortable life and never get anywhere. You can have a comfortable life after some time as a business person when you have enough income to live it. But in spite of that, a born entrepreneur just keeps going...

TEAMWORK. 25

In companies, you'll often hear the phrase "teamwork". Some new entrepreneurs worry about having a partner or employee. If you want to produce and earn money, you must create work not only for yourself but also for your employees when you have them. At the beginning, you may run your business alone, or you may only need help working at certain hours, but even so, you must be prepared to lead a team of workers. But remember, only when you need them! If you work alone in your company, you'll earn enough money to live. When they talk about "earning money", that's something you'll do when you have employees who never have nothing to do. Getting enough work for the company is the job of the company organiser.

You might ask yourself "How do I get enough customers so that I need employees?" Good question. As I said earlier, to get a lot of business, you need a lot of demand which is found in places with many inhabitants. In other words, a business which causes many people to go inside. An example: if we have a large building in a city with enough inhabitants, we coul offer a few services at a good price so that many customers come to see what we have. If we have a restaurant or café and have quite a lot of space to hold banquets (we don't necessarily need to be in the city centre for this; we could be a few kilometres away from it), many people will come along as well. Well, we'll talk about this more in the chapter about banquets.

SPONSORS.   26

There are many sponsors in sport, music, art, and so on, but who sponsors companies? Nobody! That's not true. The legion of consumers around the entire world are companies' sponsors, because without them buying our products and services, entrepreneurs and the majority of companies would not exist. This huge crowd of consumers is absolutely essential for suppliers and retailers. You can't do much without money but you can't do anything without customers.

HAVING EMPLOYEES THROUGH NECESSITY. 27

A sole businessman involved in supermarkets, electricity, catering, commerce in general or any other activity would find it impossible to do many things, sell many products or attend to all the customers in their establishment at the same time. For that reason, he needs employees.
One person doesn't have time to generate enough turnover to earn more than a standard monthly salary. Other employees are needed to produce and sell enough in order to justify the business itself. Entrepreneurs will strengthen their business when they have salaried staff. But be careful! They have to plan to know how and how much other employees' work is

required. The true business is in production and sales, whether it be products or services.

SECURITY IN THE RUNNING OF THE BUSINESS. 28

When a business has more than one partner and a firm purpose to achieve a specific aim, there is more security that there are no "leaks" or "cracks" anywhere. When one partner isn't there, the other one is, and so the business not only never stops working but also other errors which would otherwise happen can be avoided. As the business grows in size, so do the number of staff members and managers required. Sometimes, those leaks are inevitable but can be dealt with discreetly.

One thing is clear: businesses in which everyone deals with the money run the risk of someone not doing their job well and making errors when taking money. If there isn't any way to rectify this, you have to rely on luck. In busy catering businesses (such as those in large cities), if the till isn't well-controlled through receipts, there can be mistakes there too. A friend of mine who has a large catering business in Barcelona told me that when a business makes a lot of money every day, small mistakes or "leaks" don't matter so much. In any case, you should avoid them wherever possible.

With the passing of time as an entrepreneur, you'll discover that a business that doesn't need salaried staff will always be a way of earning a living independently, but you won't have money to do more than live, and you won't have time for yourself nor your family.

Who dares wins, and luck is on the side of those who aren't happy just to live. Risk-takers are the ones who don't stop trying until they get "lucky". Our vision of the future must always be one of imitating the majority of large companies. They are continuously growing, creating jobs in the new establishments they

As long as you complete any commercial action like any

other, it will always be legal. That's the law of supply and demand. When supply is high, prices are lower, and when demand is high, prices rise. If you invent or sell a product that only you have, you put a price on it.

Then, when they copy you, you'll have to be watch out for what prices your competitors put so that yours continue being competitive and selling. In any business you take part in, success all depends on your skill and intelligence. When you lose money in a business, which could happen, though not so common, don't tell anyone because they won't believe you, or they'll sympathise with pointless comments. And when you earn a lot, don't tell anyone either because they'll hate you, though they'll smile and say "you're so lucky". This is called being there through good times and bad. Your fortitude will come through them knowing as little about you as possible...

A certain level of culture for business is important, as long as it is accompanied by ingenuity and initiative. If we've got culture but no ambitions, we're done for, though we'll always complete every crossword we do! Some people don't get anywhere with anything they do. They feed off the scraps left behind by the true fighters. What happens to these people who aren't interested in anything? They dream impossible dreams and just end up reading novels instead of writing them or at least trying.

FIGHT AND WORK FOR YOUR FUTURE. 29

This fight is your best and only option. You can't be afraid since you're already involved in your future. You're your own guide and saviour. If you don't have a big inheritance or a family business to take over, you'll have to forge your own destiny. You need to start thinking what you're going to do with it starting right now. If you haven't inherited anything, you only have what you've managed to earn. Anyway, inheritances last a lot less than money you've earned yourself. We could call this long-lasting money. The only important person in the world now is you and you can't forget that your own idea are what will make you as rich and powerful as you want to be, and that it all depends on where you want to be.

We live in a world where everything is manipulated, transformed, commercialised and sold. We're immersed in a society of excessive consumption in which everything has a price. Don't you understand what I'm saying by jumping from one topic to another? I do this to make your brain work and concentrate on your objectives and priorities, those of earning money in the cleverest way you can. You've been patient to read up to here. My experience will help yo open. When we have mastered a certain activity, it's very easy to clone that business is different places. With a business like that, we'll get more and more employees and our business will grow non-stop. It wouldn't be very gratifying to sacrifice all those years working yourself if you're not well rewarded. Sometimes, if you don't have workers, you don't earn enough to justify the sacrifice of being an entrepreneur. But you'll always get more benefits working for yourself than for someone else.

SUCCESS FOLLOWS THE ASTUTE AND THE SHREWD. 30

With intelligence and self-discipline, you'll achieve the composure and mastery you need to work in industry. You have to be cool enough not to show too much interest in something you want to buy. When you're in the role of seller, you have to prove, by arguing with facts, that the quality of what you're selling is better than that of your competitors. In businesses, we always find out who can legally take the biggest advantage from what they have. In any retail operation, money can be lost by not doing your calculations right. If you can intelligently buy a product for X euros and sell it for XXXX euros, that's perfectly legal. If the reverse happens and you lose money, which also happens (though less often!), be strong. It's all part of the become more and more involved in your own project. Once you finish this book, you will have increased your knowledge about businesses, and will have the necessary security to get wherever you want to. The 2nd part of this book is about catering in general. All of the arguments I express here are totally necessary, both for those who don't know about this trade and for those who know it but haven't taken the final step. So here is my message to both groups.

YOUR KNOWLEDGE WILL HELP YOU SUCCEED. 31

Culture is important and will help you succeed but it's not essential for getting where you want to be. Knowledge of the huge range of subjects that exist has a lot to do with success but there is no hard and fast rule. Some succeed and achieve lofty goals with good preparation. Others, having had good careers, don't have the necessary willpower and end up with nothing. If they are "lucky" enough to find a dead-end job for life, they are happy. Entrepreneurs, thanks to their dynamic and ambitious characters, would like all their family members to be like them. Unfortunately this is impossible, but if you have the chance, you can try helping everyone who will listen. This book will help you. Recommend it to them, and if someone in your family reads it and decides to follow the advice in their own life, you'll be happy too. Consider it your personal achievement. There is a Jewish rule: help those who want to help themselves. The entrepreneur's mission must be the same. There's a saying: Help yourself and you will be helped.

CALLING LUCK. 32

If you chase something with all your heart, and you complete it enthusiastically, you're calling luck. Without your effort, luck won't come by itself. You have to go looking for it. Has anyone ever won the lottery without playing? Not that I know of. Entrepreneurs start a fight without an end. You will be involved in your business every day of your life, and luck will be with you throughout. People will tell you you're lucky by doing business in this way. They only see the surface. They don't understand that you get what you want with sacrifice and risks.Your good business ideas have to come from your head. Our brain is always waiting for you to make it work. Think deeply about an idea and you can change any way of working or any product. As you get used to the idea that you're being prepared for success, business ideas will pour out of you like a waterfall until you find the answer you're looking for. Write your ideas down and don't just discard any. The entrepreneur's luck is the result of the new continuous business ventures. Learning a new trade or job is starting a new business venture which will attract luck. For the experienced entrepreneur, every business you start is like rolling a snowball down a snowy mountain which becomes bigger and bigger by itself.

STARTING YOUR FIRST BUSINESS   33

When you start a business, try to be prudent and low-key to your competitors. You don't want them to see your building or business. You won't benefit at all and they will start plotting how to take you down. You might also rent other premises to use for a completely different business venture. No matter what, the less information you give, the better. You should end up setting up one which is similar to others which you will have seen before. You will copy your previous business, modifying whatever you think necessary, so that it seems a little different though has the same goal. You'll be able to announce the new opening of your future business as a new branch OPENING SOO

If you have the luck and intelligence to open a business without any competition, enjoy it while it lasts. After a short while, competitors will appear. Before opening a business in a certain place, keep an eye on any similar ones near to where you'll put yours. Go in like a regular customer without making it too obvious you're looking around. You'll see that many of the things there will be worth copying and improving in your business. After you've opened the business, visiting these places to spy on them would be shameless. Instead, you could invite them to your opening if it seems appropriate. If your business is doing well, don't just stop trying, thinking that the money will fly in without any more effort on your part. A good business is the result of good ideas, realised with skill and the desire to achieve it.

DO WHATEVER WILL GET PEOPLE IN YOUR PREMISES. 34

When you start a business, if you are a direct sale company, you have to get customers into your shop on opening day, even if you give them something for free. It could be wine or another drink, a calendar, or anything else which costs little. It depends on the business you open. To begin with, it could be that nobody knows your business. Don't wait until years have passed. You have to do everything in your power to let the whole city know your company exists and what you are selling. In the first few days, you'll end up giving away a lot of your profits. That doesn't matter. Advertising is the modern weapon for selling more. Don't underestimate it.

They used to say "Good wine needs no bush". This meant

that you didn't have to advertise if your product is good. People will buy it anyway. But this is no longer true. A product, service or business becomes popular through publicity, and it begins working from the opening day.

You've seen plenty of advertising in magazines, on TV and in other media. They sometimes show half-naked women in order to sell anything. These are psychological tricks used to appeal to potential customers' base instincts. You have to learn as much as you can from others because otherwise it will take you a lot longer to get where you want to be.

You have to get people into your shops, even if you do it by giving sweets to children. The first time they come into your shop, it will be due to an invitation or gift. The second and following times will be much simpler because they know where you are and know what they will find. After that, it's a question of making them come back. Many people will come in to see if they can find what they want, willing to spend money. The entrepreneur needs to ensure that these customers leave their money and walk out happy.

DON'T SCRIMP ON PUBLICITY.   35

Advertising will tell people about your company from day one. If you don't spend on advertising, people will take longer in finding out you exist. Be careful: first, you need to understand what you're doing. Publicity may be harmful if you're not able to deal with the amount of customers that come. Can you imagine if some company offered a new service or product at a really cheap price, the people are queuing up outside and end up waiting because there are hardly any staff available? Customers wouldn't get the attention they need or wouldn't be able to buy the product or service, and they would end up speaking badly about the business. This counter-productive publicity must be avoided at all costs. When you offer a popular, cheap product, you have to make sure you have enough for the first day, even if you lose money as a result.

These "hook" products, sold at cost price, can be advertised in a controlled manner, only letting people know about them, or offering them only for a short period of time, or only "while stocks last". In this last case, you remove the sign and that's the end of it. Then you can decide if it's worth putti another product or service on offer. In this way, you publicise the business and the result is that more products are sold than expected. I'm generalising here, and not talking much about catering. To give a relevant example, one day, you could offer a free pudding with every meal. The range of businesses is extremely wide as we will see in other chapters.

KNOW WHAT OTHERS ARE DOING   36

Learn about real life. As in school, college or university, you have to memorise everything that passes before your eyes. Your brain is always waiting for you to give it some information. If you already know what business you want to do but you've never done it before, offer to work in a company of that type, regardless of the type of work. What matters is that you get in and understand how it works. Everything you learn will help you start your own business.

Starting a business with some experience is important in order to develop it well. You can also start up collaborating with someone who does have experience, whether they are an employee or for an agreed price. If you have the project in your head while you're working for others, you will always have the chance to learn. Never tell anyone about your goals, not your work colleagues, not even your best friend. If you tell you want to learn in order to start up your own business, the bosses will find out and you may be sacked before you learn the business. Go into that company as a worker, trying to be the best and seeing whatever you can.

A future entrepreneur who works in a company will not miss the chance to gather data or addresses of suppliers for all products which are used. Never stop gathering all the information you can; you won't be the first nor the last to do it. With this knowledge, be alert, when you are an entrepreneur, to guard your secrets. When you start your first business, you start to forge your future as an entrepreneur as long as you apply yourself with a lot of willpower. If your budget allows you to start a business but you've never done it before, do what I did. Look for a professional as an employee or adviser for an agreed price ahead of time, so they can help you start up the business. If you use your head before opening the business, things usually turn out well.

ISPONSORS. 37

Having employees through necessity.Security in the running of the business.Fight and work for your future. Success follows the astute and the shrewd 19
Your knowledge will help you succeed.Calling luck. Starting your first businessDo whatever will get people in your premises.Don't scrimp on publicity.Know what others are doing Internal movement.

INTERNAL MOVEMENT. 38

You should take an employee only when you need one. There has to be work for everyone in a business, even for the boss. There's no point in having employees twiddling their thumbs, or bosses or managers giving a bad example. In that case, the business would go to ruin. You should understand that one person alone will never be able to do enough work to make a big profit.

They need more pairs of hands to manufacture or create the

products, such as a cook in a restaurant or bar, and shop assistants or waiters help to sell products. This is achieved with teamwork. Creating demand for products or services requires imagination while working.

The owner of a company will gain more profit by creating work for his employees. Find ways to create products in less time and at a lower cost to be more competitive. Services in cafés and similar business should be done quickly and carefully, prices agree with the type of business, and the customers notice how clean your establishment is when they visit. This
is all achieved by creating and training a good team.

In fact, you should always aim to have too much work so that there is no dead space. That's why mass production was created. When creating a product, every employee creates a different part of the same product, until it is finished and packaged. The size of the workshop doesn't matter. If this form of working isn't implemented, you won't get the resu we want and you won't get the proper benefits. When talking about catering, you still have to behave as if it were a factory.

Every employee must have their responsibility. Everything the boss can't do will be delegated to the best possible person. You need to predict what you will need the next day and make sure you have in available ahead of time. Refill the store or at least make the order with the supplier for the next day.

YOU NEVER KNOW HOW FAR YOU CAN GET. 39

A person never knows how far they are capable of getting until they try it out. There are many people who work double shifts without any problems. Some work 15 hours a day or more without taking a day off for years. No self-employed worker has fixed hours. Working long hours every day can be a way of improving your money situation. This is easy to achieve if you train your body to do what your brain tells it to do. You won't feel any pain. On the contrary, you'll feel happy when you see your income rising.

LIMITATION OF COMMAND. 40

When you place trust in an employee, giving them certain responsibilities, and they don't show themselves as up to the task, you'll have to change their work role. This change can be traumatic for both parties and the business has nothing to gain from this. When you hand out responsibilities, you have to be sure you're choosing the right person. A good, responsible worker, when he is well-paid for his efficiency and attachment to the company, pass this on to his colleagues. If the reverse happens to an employee and you find that your working environment is being undermined, it's better to end the situation as soon as possible.

The longer it takes to resolve, the more money and problems it will cause the business. Entrepreneurs can't accept their business failing for lack of discipline and efficiency and this isn't always achieved with a good salary. When a member of our body is sick and can't be cured, if it isn't amputated in time, the rest of the body will die. It's the same in businesses. Amputation in time is a victory, since anything else would be dangerous. The manager's responsibilities must be fair so that they don't start running a dictatorship. Apart from the fact that it would be too much for them, the owner runs the risk of losing control. Remember the old saying: "Give them an inch and they'll take a mile".

THE MANAGER AND THEIR MISSION. 40.A

Among the employees, you'll find various trustworthy people who efficiently complete any task you give them. Other important responsibilities that the manager has are: organising the team to do what they should be doing; always being on top of production and staff; and the development of maintenance and hygiene. There can be no business in which the expenditure and staff levels be higher than those established, otherwise the business will lose its profitability. The company would become bankrupt since it would have more money going out than coming in. A business is started with the aim of gaining money. The obligation to create jobs in society belongs to the government. They have to come up with a good national economic plan so that businesses can grow and create job positions. However, businessmen help the situation when the economic circumstances allow it. It all depends on the government's economic administration of its people

THE COMPLETE POWER OF THE COMPANY 41

Discipline and working rules will determine the boss and manager from the very beginning of the business. It all has to be decided in advance, because otherwise, it will be much harder later and cause no end of problems. However, you will discover new ways to work and develop simply through experience gained through day-to-day work. If employees see their boss being lazy, slow and disorganised, they'll learn to work in the same way. They'll always do what they see others doing. If they do what they should, anyone who <u>doesn't like it</u> will get bored and leave.

When you hear people say that in a certain company, big or small, it's hard work, those companies work well and make money. When you hear the opposite, that the employees are comfortable, the company won't last long. Over time, I've seen that when the manager is slow, in certain sets of jobs, every other employee will follow the same rhythm. This is resolved from the first moment, setting a rhythm which no-one can interrupt. If anyone goes at a different speed, it could interrupt the pace of the whole business.

Never give one person all responsibilities. Only certain parts of the company should be under one person's charge. An employee can never hire nor fire another on a whim or because they don't get on. It would be confusing and dangerous. Cliques could be formed which would never help the business.

If you don't want to take risks when it comes to employees, learn all you can about the relevant laws and put them into practice, even before you start working.

Businesses of a good size work better if responsibilities are given out to in groups to different staff, or they put their accounting department in charge of employees joining or leaving the company as an extra task. If the company is small, it's worth them having a legal agency to work with so that any problem can be efficiently resolved by their lawyer.

.....

INFLUENCES AND THEIR EFFECTS. 42

I always say that you should keep your relatives separate from your company. If you are a dynamic, hard worker, other people who don't work so hard may come to see if they can benefit from you without working so hard. It could be anyone, but if you have a bad worker who is family (something which you'll discover it's too late), it'll be more difficult to resolve the matter. They may think that being related to you, your wife or a business partner, they don't have to work so hard. These problems are resolved in advance if we don't allow family members to join the company. Recommendations that don't work out because the person doesn't work hard put both the boss of the company and the one who made the recommendation in a difficult situation. An advantage of the freedom we have is that we can have whatever employees are suitable without having being stifled by compromises. The only exception is that there could be a family member who we know is good and so is good for the company.

ADVERTISING. 43

I've advertised in various ways, and every method I've used that worked well was because I found a professional to implement it for me. On some occasions, I hired someone to do it and other times, it was an employee. As such, I recommend to any future entrepreneur that you find someone to help you do this, in whatever capacity. They should have good references or you should have seen them working. When I started a restaurant-café, on the opening day, the bar was busy for the entire day. Some customers paid, others didn't. A few days earlier, we had given out invitations in shopping malls and offices nearby. That day was incredibly busy. Most of the customers without invitations left without paying. A large amount percentage of the city drank for free. The waiters had practically no time to serve and take money.

When I had planned this before starting this campaign, I knew that something like that could happen because I'd heard it happen in another catering business, but I had never imagined such an amount of people. There were those who said I didn't need to do so much advertising. What I'm sure of is that I never regretted it. I made sure that a large amount of people knew about the Aragón Restaurant-Café situated at 28 Alfonso Street, Zaragoza. Good location, central and full of tourists, near to the Basilica of Our Lady of the Pillar.

Advertising brought that about deliberately and it bore results. The days that followed were good, and sales continued as if the business had been going forever. We gained a lot of regular customers. These new customers had gone to other nearby businesses before, so we took clientele from our competitors. That is competition. It's very important, when you start a business of any type, to give it the appropriate publicity. In catering in particular, having a day with a free bar might cost you some money, but the business will thank you for it. Of course, there are other methods of advertising.

RHYTHM FROM THE FIRST DAY. 44

The rhythm of working has to push your workers according to the type of business you have. If it is based on selling a lot at low prices, it has to work like a factory in mass production. If the products and business are higher-class, the rhythm will be slower, since the product on sale will be more expensive, and more time will be taken over making sales. This doesn't mean that the service shouldn't be sufficiently dynamic. Don't wait for that rhythm to be set by just anyone there. You should find the perfect employee for the role and pay them enough for their efficiency to be your standard from the first day.

ON EXPENSES AND STOCK. 45

The general costs of your business will be the salaries for anyone in the business and all costs incurred for any reason that helps the business. These include: rent, insurance, salaries and fees, publicity, electricity, telephone, water, stationery, cleaning products, wrapping material for your products, transport, taxes, repairs, loans and interest, tools, legal or accounting fees, etc. It's necessary to prevent, or at least calculate, every general cost which you may have in a year before starting the business. However, you may not be able to determine the exact amounts until the year finishes. Stock which you buy in order to re-sell is something different. Any profits you may get through sales will depend on you being able to pay those costs. Even business has a different size and class, in terms of its general expenses. In a small company in which there are only one or two people, these expenses may be small. Sales made will be appropriate to that type of company. On the other hand, even having more employees in that same business, if the production is increased, the general expenses will be reduced, assuming the same costs on rent, and so on.

PAYING EMPLOYEES WITH PROFITS. 46

It has been shown that rewarding sales or employee production causes sales or production to increase and the company to get more money. The general expenses will be the same or almost the same. An example: a salesman manages to sell €100 in a day. If they get 35 percent of what they sell, they will clearly earn 35 euros (gross) that day. If we give the salesman a certain percentage increase in this amount, sales will increase. It's just an example which you would have to calculate. In calculating your expenses, let's suppose that the first one or two hundred euros, however much you might get, covers your costs completely.

The real profits earned in the company are gained from the total of sales made. When all your employees' sales cover the general expenses for that day, you make a profit. Commission is necessary in catering, much as in any other type of business, although it's a little different because it is shared among all employees. If the waiters got commission and the chefs didn't, the waiters could sell much more (assuming the cooks would help them out by making the food). The best thing is to share commission between both groups, since it's worth paying a certain percentage to those who work extra so the company doesn't lose any money.

If staff are given extra benefits for working well, they'll work harder and more happily, and there will be a more competitive atmosphere between employees. The employee must understand their importance to the company and the reason you're paying them commission. It's neither convenient nor necessary to give much explanation about the business and its administrative section to any employee or person who is not an interested party. Throughout the year, some days will have fewer sales which will be compensated for by the busier days. I've always worked in large cities with many inhabitants, which is why I always talk about competition and large amounts of sales. This wouldn't happen in a villages or small towns where your only competition is in you giving a good service.

In catering, as a general rule, 30% of the total sales will go towards stock, 30% towards general expenses, and the other 40% is profit before taxes. The result can be alarming when numbers of sales are too low. The truth is that the profits have to be fairly high, because there are unforeseen costs of all types. For example, if you work with seafood and they don't sell, they'll go off and have to be thrown away. In catering in general, you will work with products which come with a certain risk, which is why it's usual to put such high profit margins, over 35%, on certain products. When giving out commission, it must be done according to the rank and salary of each employee. When a shirt or pair of shoes goes out of fashion, you reduce the price to sell them without making a loss, but there is no risk that they might break, like crockery or machinery which, when they break, need to be replaced or repaired.

GENERALISING INCENTIVES NEVER GIVES GOOD RESULTS. 47

In some business sectors, they may be extra benefits besides commission. You must do the calculations and know when and who to give these benefits to, since generalising never gives good results. There are good workers who are efficient even without getting any benefits. There are others who have a good salary but have to be encouraged and not let out of your sight, making sure they have enough to do. There are people who, if you reward them without explanation, might think that the business does it because it's suitable for them, or they are making a lot of money. Those that are rewarded without explanation will take it as their right which will later be difficult to rectify job....

PREVIOUS JOBS, 48

Many entrepreneurs without a job start thinking they could start working for themselves while looking for another job. In such cases, they don't have the slightest idea that in doing other jobs which you've never thought about before, they start opening other doors which, in time, will make them into businessmen.

When this restlessness is awakened, it's the most important moment of their life. Something is activated in their brain and they start acting according to their thoughts. It's common that experience from previous jobs, posts or trades will help the future entrepreneur as a base for starting their own first business. In this book, you'll discover that luck is with you, and that you'll find the starting point in catering or any other profession, even if you've never done it before.

CHAPTER 2   49

OPENING A PUB.   50

There are as many catering businesses as we want to create. They can be of any type. It depends on the money we want to spend. The first thing we see when you look at a pub is the bar, tables, chairs, café and little else. The bar must be connected to the kitchen which will simplify the business's service. The toilets mustn't be situated in places near to other private parts of the business. You have to put them in places where the customers can go directly. At the most, a short passage with no access to other areas of the building.

LET'S START WITH THE BARS. 51

There are various materials used to build a bar. You'll never see two bars the same, neither with the same materials nor the same height and width. Some are made of brick with a cover of wood, stainless steel, ceramic, tiles, or any other material that could be used. Others are made in a workshop on one piece, or various pieces which are they assembled in the pub. The most important part to take into account is the counter where the drinks are placed. On average, it should be about 50 cm wide, with space for small windows to put some food or snacks on show for the customers, leaving a little space in front of these to serve the customers.
The best height for serving the customers will is approximately 1.2 m, but actually there is no definite measurement. You'll see totally different heights and widths in every establishment you visit. When you plan a business of this type, you have to take your time and study it first. Look at everything through your customers' eyes, paying attention to comfort for both customers and staff. Make it as

good as possible while practical. It should be comfortable for customers and waiters, as this will get you more sales. You can read about other businesses in the chapter on cafés.

Before starting, we need to speak to where the ideal locations are, according to the type of business. This is something we'll speak about in more depth later in the book. Wooden counters covered in plastic are cheap but not recommended since they burn, break or scratch easily. You can copy the height and width of the bar from other pubs or restaurants. Take a measuring tape with you in your pocket and take the measurements.Some people who make them very high so customers can't lean on them and others less so, so they can. This reminds me of a newspaper stand where, before buying something, you would be disappointed if you tried to read any front pages, because som newsagents put them upside down so you couldn't read them. I never bought anything from these stands. They don't know how to make their customers happy before buying. They're bad businessmen.

THE WALLS OF THE PUB. 52

The most elegant restaurants have light-coloured walls, painted every year. In pubs and cafés in areas with lots of customers, they may be painted so that they are easy to wash, but the most practical is to use ceramic, up to a metre and a half or two metres from the floor, and not in loud colours. You could also use marble, depending on how much you want to spend. What matters is that they can be cleaned easily. With a wet or damp cloth, they can look like new every day. If they aren't cleaned frequently, they'll get darker and lose its shine. The upper parts of the walls and rooms can be painted with light, happy colours. Painting can be done in one night, and it's not necessary to close the place to paint it. The wall where the bottles of spirits are located should be ceramic, since it's the part of the wall where the bartender's back is when serving customers. It should be around 1.5 m from the ground, with shelves for bottles around the same height as the bar.

GENTS TOILETS. 53

These must be equipped with at least one stall, running water and toilet paper. Upon entering, there should also be a urinal, sink, mirror, and either an electric hand dryer or paper towels. They all need ventilation to allow gases to escape.

LADIES TOILETS. 54

The same as above and, if there is space, a shelf, next to the sink or separate, so that the ladies can place their bag on or change a baby's nappy. You will lose good customers if you have horrible toilets. The size should be in relation to the size of the building and the relevant municipal laws. The bigger and better the premises, the better the class and number of customers you have, the more space your toilets should have. As for how they are laid out, we'd all like to have a say but... The technical architect will decide, or the technician that completes the job, in agreement with the entrepreneur. When the premises are new, the technician will create the plans which have to be presented at the town hall so they can give permission to build and open the establishment. If the business is already open and has to be partially refurbished, they only need to change the name and the necessary work. As most, they would need to get permission to do some minor work but there is no need for plans. When you only need minor internal refurbishment, there are people who will do it without need for permission. The final word belongs to the technician or owner of the business.

TOILETS AND CUSTOMERS. 55

When a new business is opened, everything must be gleaming. The toilets will deteriorate with use, even if you clean them well every day. After four or five years, the toilets may be visibly deteriorated and darkened with time. If this happens, it's a good idea to do them from scratch. If you start a business by renting a pub, you should bear in mind that, as well as the refurbishments or repairs you think are necessary, you start completely refurbish the toilets from scratch, unless it has already been done for you. The customers are the ones who keep the business going by turning up, and if they complain every time they go to the bathroom, something is wrong. You have to keep the customers happy when they go to the toilet. That way, the will come back and visit us again, and their wallets will open like flowers, making our till bloom. You have to pay the government taxes on any declared profits. The costs for these jobs are taken from your income as business costs, so they will be deducted from your taxes, as I explain in this book.

TOILETS AND CHANGING ROOMS FOR EMPLOYEES. 56

It's usual to have toilets for men and women separately. These should include a stall. Sinks, mirrors, towels and soap, a normal shower and a lockable locker for each employee. Each is in relation of the size of the business. The technician will know what is correct according to the size or type of business. On the other hand, the town hall's health department will have the final word. You should ask the question at the town hall before completing the job, not after. If you work with a quantity surveyor or technical architect, he'll know what is required by law.

STOREROOM FOR STOCK. 57

If we want to control the stock that we have and that we have and receive in the company, it's good to have a room with a lock in which you can store bottles, food and other products in the business. If the business is small and rigorous control is a nuisance, you better make sure that nobody goes in who shouldn't be there. There should be shelves and space enough to pile up boxes of drinks. When the stock arrives, if you haven't prepared the packages because they're in the store and you can't see the suppliers at that moment, tell them to leave it in a place out of the way, outside of the storeroom. You won't sell that stock on that day. You can sort it out later and prepare it for next time. The aim is that no-one goes into the storeroom that shouldn't be there. You must avoid temptation.

MINIMUM EQUIPMENT REQUIRED IN THE KITCHEN OF THE PUB. 58

We can leave the size of the premises undetermined since hardly any premises are the same size. There are pieces of equipment used in some business which aren't in others, though there are always some essentials. A pub, as small as it might be, must have a small kitchen where certain items of food can be prepared.

You must have an extractor fan, a cooker, a fridge to hold the food, a large sink, a work counter, casserole dishes, good shelves for dishes and cutlery, frying pans, a machine for slicing cold meats, a variety of pans, electric whisk, knives, a discreet place for the bin, and other cooking equipment. There should also be a larder or pantry for food you use every day, some distance from the heat of the cooker. If there is a deep fryer, you can deep-fry most of the food, apart from the fish, chorizos and other food that may leave its taste behind.

The cooker can be electric or gas, but it's better to have one which is mixed so that if one goes off, we have the other. The oven can also be electric or gas, for grilled meat, pastas and various other things.In the sales area, as well as the bar, you can have a sink under the counter, shelves for glasses and dishes, a bottle fridge at arm height, a grill, a microwave for fast food at the counter when there is no-one else in the kitchen so we don't have to leave the bar, a coffee maker, coffee grinder, and other things you'll find as you go along. In the counter area and on the walls at the back of the waiter when he is in front of the customers, you can put the coffee maker and grinder, the till, and anything else suitable.

When you set out the kitchen, leave free space for unforeseen equipment. Remember that the extractor fan should remove the air completely and not redistribute it into the public area. The extractor fan is, of course, obligatory and necessary in any kitchen. In the area where the customers are, you should install a small extractor fan if you have a grill for fast food at the bar. There are many other tools you might need depending on the business. If a commercial installation contractor sets everything out for you, they will know what you need depending on your business. When setting up this type of business, the company that sells you the equipment will want to sell you as much as possible. Be careful. If they sell you things you don't need, you can end up drowning in useless investments. Buy only the essentials, and then you can buy later whatever you need.

.A COLLABORATOR TO HELP START THE BUSINESS. 59

If you haven't worked in the trade, you should hire a professional who knows it well even if it is only for starting up the business, because if you think you'll be able to get by without help, you're wrong. If you're planning to work alone for the moment, look for someone to help you who understands what you want so they can help you, and it'll be the best investment you can make in that business. If you need another person to help you in the kitchen, look for a woman who knows how to work in a pub kitchen, and you, as the owner, can be the face of the business who deals with the customers. (Even if you're a chef.) If you are a chef, you can teach them what you know, but don't let someone else be the face of the business.

THE TILL. 60

It should be away from the public. When you choose to how lay out the business, leave a space for the till which could be on a wall which is at the back of your staff when they are dealing with a customer, or wherever is most convenient. It's a good idea to have the screen on top of the till showing the amount to pay on view, a metre above the till. The customers see what they have to pay better from a distance which has a psychological effect, which is healthy for your business. If you take part physically in your job as the owner and you're also a cook, attend customers in the bar. Even if you're a cook, the business will succeed or fail
based on the service customers receive and how their money is handled. They'll do what you tell them to in the kitchen since you know what you're talking about. If the business has lots of customers and various employees, get a manager or supervisor who will earn commission on sales. Whether the business works will partly depend on him or her, but they'll always know their responsibilities and you'll be sure that they're the person you want in charge. Every business is a type of machine, which only works if all the nuts and bolts are tightened and in the right place. Of course, your profits come from taking money. If you have a black hole in your

till, your future won't look very promising. You need to take good care of your till. Many hands working and only the correct ones taking money.

The screen on the till is one idea for a promotion. Another is that the receipt be numbered and dated and to the lucky winner whose numbers match with the particular lottery, a prize! What prize? Make it up. They could get double their change back or whatever occurs to you, without overstepping the boundaries of being sensible while being something worth winning. The majority won't even look but every time you give a prize, raise your voice and announce: "Prize for so-and-so who wins such-and-such". It's all good publicity.

The inhabitants of the village, area or city you're in have to know that your business exists. You've already started down the path to success and luck. To sell more every day, you have to spend some time thinking, copying ideas and improving or inventing them, because no-one else will do it for you. The furniture in a pub depends on the place anamount of space available in the premises. Tables and chairs and some bar stools. We'll talk about this later with other catering businesses.

SELLING SANDWICHES. 61

If your business is situated on a busy, commercial street and you want to sell a lot of sandwiches, you have to do it very well. Study the final cost of various types of sandwiches, rolls and fillings. The different ways to prepare them are endless - as many as you can think of. The best thing is to do a selection and study ten or fifteen of the most common ones that look good to you. Ones that are easy and quick to make and organise. You have to do the calculations yourself and put the same amount of filling for each one. If you group the sandwiches into price bands, you'll work quickly and efficiently. You can earn lots of money with sandwiches and sell many because they are so quick to make. I always tell entrepreneurs that they should think like factories in everything they do in their business.

If the sandwiches go well, it can be a very good business. Put in public view inside your bar a numbered list of all the sandwiches and their prices, another copy of the list in your kitchen so they can be produced quickly, and a third in front of the business for passers-by to see. Having these numbers, the kitchen will be a factory ready to take orders by number. This is the secret to selling lots of sandwiches. With everything I've said, success depends on the speed of the services and the area of the city you're in. In all cities, there is always a popular commercial sector in which the prices are very high because there are so many people who go in these shops. Premises in the right place, even if they are expensive, can make you rich. And one if you open one in an area with few customers, even if the rent is cheap, you run the risk of losing everything you put into it.

SANDWICH SIGN.   62

Example of a sign for the front of a business: It can be made of wood or panelling, about 40 cm wide and approximately a metre tall, painted white. Mount this in a frame painted red or blue which will stand out, 1.50 cm wide all around the board. The entire sign has vertical and horizontal stripes about 4 mm thick like a grid, the same colour as the frame. The white squares in between these lines could be 10 cm wide by seven tall (these are examples which you can improve). In each square, write, using paint, what each sandwich has inside. In one of the corners, put the number of the sandwich in small digits. Leave a white or light space to put the price with chalk or a wax pencil which can be easily erased, followed by the word "euros" or the currency in your country written in the same paint as above. This job has to be done with competitive prices so that you sell a lot and make your business into a sandwich factory. Success will come only if you plan everything beforehand. Specific example. In the sign and its squares, you could put, for example: Fried calamari and mayonnaise, X euros. Dry-cured ham and slices of tomato.

Cooked ham and cheese with mayonnaise. French omelette with slices of tomato or mayonnaise. Hot-dog with pickles, etc., etc. We could carry on inventing and we would fill pages and pages. Wherever you go, keep your eyes open, and you'll see ways to improve your products. This sign must be completed by a professional, similar to the one mentioned at the end of these chapters. The painter should have a sketch or an idea of what they are going to do before starting. Make sure they have clearly written what needs to go in each square. This sign will cost a bit of money to make but will be worth it. You'll just need to change the price in chalk or wax pencil whenever you want. The price can be written in euros or whatever the currency of you country, for each sandwich or portion.

(SANDWICH SIGN EXAMPLE ON NEXT PAGE)   63

These signs give the place a sense of style and help you sell more. It's one way of turning your company into a sandwich factory. The writing describing the contents of the sandwiches should be written in block capitals, so that they can be easily read. Make your own cost calculations and don't worry about what other people sell. Just make sure that yours <u>are no more expensive</u> than those of your competitors.

The painter will show you a few styles of letters. Choose the one which is easiest to read. A list of sandwiches made on the spot along with their contents can be found at the end of this chapter. The advantages of having these signs are that the price can be changed and you can wash them, and they'll always look like new. This is something I strongly recommend for you to make money. If you can't serve a particular sandwich on one day because you don't have an ingredient, cross it out with chalk so customers know there aren't any (ten or fifteen years with a sandwich company in a busy area with lots of customers should be enough to save for a good retirement). But it has to have a good location

FROZEN BREAD ROLLS. 64

Success in this industry depends on the bread being fresh and soft, and that you don't have too much nor not enough. Of course it's always to have too much bread than have to say: "We don't have any sandwiches because there's no bread left." (For the bread that's left over, we can use that too.) You should have the ideal oven which can keep on cooking whatever is needed. These days, bakers produce bread whose dough is frozen and ready to bake. The order you make for bread, confectionery and pastries, if you also do breakfasts, is usually made the night before. You should ask for some baked bread to sell immediately, and other necessary or frozen products. Electric oven can be set at different levels and are very simple to use. Whoever you get the oven from can show you how to use it if necessary. Sometimes the bakers themselves will install the oven for free. If you are original, you can make a lot of money in sandwiches. People get tired of burgers them but also have twenty other types. On previous pages, I described how to make a sign with a strong impact on customers to increase your sales. This sign, or one very similar which you've designed yourself using my advice, will make your business into a mass producing sandwich factory. It will never fail if take my advice on how to build it and where to put it. How will you make it effective? Every business has its own secrets to success. They are the result of studying the area we're located in well and the customers we're aiming at.

SANGRIA AND AN INVITATION. 65

Advertising to sell a lot! It's quite common to see signs in some catering businesses which say: "Come and taste our house sangria for free", or whatever else. (Or whatever you've invented until others copy you) You can be the first to try it in this place. Invite to have a "little glass" of sangria and put up a sign with the price per litre. It's all publicity to get more customers. Making it is really easy: A transparent glass jug filled halfway with cold red wine, three or four spoonfuls of sugar mixed in, a splash of lemonade or other fizzy drink, or lemon or orange juice.
Two shots of spirits or the remains of the bottles from your shelves. A few slices of lemon, orange, ripe peaches or syrup. This should be prepared and left to cool or made with cold wine, or you have it already prepared in the fridge. When you serve it, top it up with ice to the brim, put a wooden spoon in so customers can serve themselves. You can add lemon or orange peel, or something similar, partly in the jug with the rest hanging out. If you fill it with ice too early before serving it, "the sangria will be watered down". So make sure you have it prepared and cold before, and only add the ice just before you serve it. By doing this, you can be sure that the product will be cold and the customers will like it. It's a psychological act which will please the customers.

MINI CANAPÉS AND LOW COST TAPAS. 66

Tapas in pubs give good results. You have to advertise them one way or another. You can give make a sign and give it to them as a page in a menu, or with a thick felt-tip pen, stuck with a drawing pin to a wall. Or done well using a computer to be more presentable.

They are all promotional materials used to increase your business's sales. You could put "Free tapas today" on a sign and put it up and take it down whenever you want. Remember that you have to plan it all so it goes well. They have to be original and low-cost, since you'll lose money if you give away excellent food. Do it well and your sales will grow.

There are really simple things like potatoes. Cut them into slices, boil them in three to five minutes, keep them in the fridge and they're ready to be served in portions. When they need it, throw them in a frying pan, cook them with really hot oil and they're done in no time. Put them on a plate with some spicy mayonnaise. For the promotional free tapas, put a slice of potato for each customer, put a little bit of spicy sauce on top, stick a cocktail stick in it and serve. You can sell them in good-sized portions too but don't put the prices too low. Another possibility is diced potatoes stewed with veal bone and spices, arranged well on the plate. Put them on a saucer with some sauce or with a cocktail stick. You could also make fried fish fritters, made on the spot and served with a cocktail stick. There should be two or three with different varieties, enough that the customer asks for a full portion. Remember that they should be ordering portions of these tapas and calculate the sale price beforehand.

You've already cast your hook out - don't forget to decide the price, quality and quantity per portion. If you're tight with your portions, they might get one but no more. If you're more generous without going over the top, you'll sell and earn more and more every day.If you sow your seeds intelligently, you'll have a good harvest. Another low-cost tapa: a small slice of tomato with chopped onion on top, a few drops of olive oil, sprinkle with pepper, and serve with a cocktail stick. People who have worked in a pub kitchen can make a huge variety of tapas.

You're the one that has to say which to give away and which to sell. If the sign says: "A free tapa of your choice when you buy three tapas of the day per purchase", in another sign, you have to write what the tapas of the day are. Your customers will quickly get used to free food, so you have to change the variety every now and then. This is something easy to do but you'll notice a big difference when it comes to the money you're taking in which, for the business, is the most important thing. It will be even better if you have a decent range of tapas at normal prices. This is called pushing your business onwards. If the business doesn't have any initiative, it's just another one on the pile. If you're in an excellent location, the sales will come automatically. But even so, having initiative will make a huge difference.counter. Others have tables which the customer can use after having paid for and received what they want at the counter. The food is usually wrapped in paper or plastic. These businesses sell a lot if their prices are average without being competitive. Almost everything that you sell should be on display or in signs which show what you're offering.

The grill should be on view because the whole business is one. When there's a lot of work on, the best thing is for one person to stay at the grill making whatever the other staff tell them to (or the staff member who takes the order does it himself). Working like this in mass production helps ease matters. Working slowly will lose you sales. The customers will be thankful and when they see you working well, they'll keep coming back. In some summer destinations, the working season is often very short. In others, such as Tenerife or the south of Las Palmas in the Canary Islands, there is tourism all year round.

This also happens in areas with historical monuments, like the Basilica in Zaragoza, Santiago de Compostela Cathedral in Galicia, Alhambra in Granada in Spain, etc. Around these monuments, both restaurants and gift shops work every day of the year. In these businesses with many visitors, the range of products has to be very wide and uncomplicated. There could be hot sandwiches to make on the spot, such as meat, burgers, sausages, cold meats, cheese, etc. French fries served hot in paper cones sell well too. You need a good range of sandwiches you can make quickly, and others with cold meats ready to take away, as well as ice-cream, drinks, beer and soft drinks in cans, etc.

Although there are some people who will eat at the counter, serve those behind those customers at the counter so that they can take their food and drinks, pay and take them away. These businesses work like in fairs. They take the money before giving the food to the customer, otherwise people would leave without paying. This system is used wherever there are many customers.

PUBS WITH FOOD IN TOURIST AREAS. 67

When we are tourists, we're like wandering birds that walk the streets. When we see a place nearby that looks good, we find the first table and seat available to rest and drink something. Some of these businesses have terraces with tables outside. There are also those that have a dining room inside with food service. The prices usually aren't competitive. They range from acceptable to expensive. These visiting customers apparently think that it's just a one-off thing and not think about it, but they may come back a few days and other years. Customers, if you treat them well and give good service, don't forget easily. You know what they do forget? The price, if the food, treatment and service were good.

These companies are combine harvesters, reaping every day.

If you don't sow any seeds, there'll be nothing to harvest. The prices may be expensive, but if you have a list in view of the customers with the prices, you're not fooling anyway. What's bad is charging more, or some people more, others less, because that's where confusion comes from. If you charge people just when you see them, it will be confusing.

When a customer enters, sometimes you won't remember if you charged them for a beer the last time they came in. If you think you're selling something too cheaply, change it in the list, but always charge the same to all customers. If you have tables, you can serve food. Combination platters are profitable and you can store them half-cooked. (Read more in the chapter on cafés.) Even so, you can have some freshly cooked food too. What isn't good for you, if you're busy and have little space, is à la carte cooking.

GIVING AWAY SOMETHING FOR FREE ALWAYS GIVES GOOD RESULTS. 68

Don't forget that nobody gives away anything for nothing. If a beer costs you one X and you sell it for three XXX, what does it matter if you take away a bar from one of the three Xs and we sell them for a lower price than other pubs? Or if we give away a free tapa with every drink? Doing this, your sales will increase. The truth is that at the end of the day, instead of selling three boxes of beer, you'll have sold five, the staff and rent will be the same, and the costs will be very similar. Nobody apart from the owner will do these promotions (because their workload will increase).

If you can get more sales with the same general costs, you get more profits. If the prices are correct according to the service and quality, the public will get used to it and come back time and time again. If the sales increase so much you need another staff member, go ahead and keep selling more because that's only good for your business. If you do all this in a desert <u>or a place with very few people</u>, you won't get good results and this book will have been for nothing

THE WEEKLY DAY OF REST. 69

Everything has its advantages and disadvantages. There are industrial areas in which there are very few people on certain days in which you may as well close and have a day off. In other areas, you sell more at weekends and won't close any day of the year. It would be best for the business and employees to have a day off during the week. At weekends, if the amount of work goes up, look for extra staff to help those who normally work those days.

DIFFERENT TYPES OF CATERING BUSINESSES. 70
For those that don't know the trade, almost all pubs look the sam The truth is that they change depending on their location. Among the various types of job in catering that exist, the times at which they are busiest are completely different, save the dinner hour. Some are in the city centre surrounding by shops. Others are in the outskirts of cities or smaller towns or villages. In tourist zones, summer holiday locations, industrial areas, office areas, etc. Some will have plenty of tables because they'll make most of their sales to people sitting down, while others have lots of customers but not much space and so few tables, which means most of their sales are made at the counter. It all depends on the space available and the location of your business. Every business has its focus set according to its location and customers. In many businesses, all types of people go in and so it's essential to give a good service to attract more customers every day. There are those who look at the customer and charge according to what they see. These people exist in all types of businesses and their future is decided by their behaviour.

There are tourist areas in which prices are higher because their season is short. The best thing for the business is to charge the same prices to both and hot dogs all the time. You can have tourists and locals.

TAPAS PUBS.   71

These businesses work very well in commercial areas since there are so many people. They need to have all the services normal pubs offer, such as spirits, beers and lagers, soft drinks, meals, tapas, snacks, sandwiches, etc. Quite a few pubs of this type offer three-course meals or just a combination platter at meal times. The display windows in the bar should be filled with varieties of what you offer the customers: tapas served cold or to be heated, portions of food, ready-made sandwiches, cold meats, pastries for breakfasts, etc. This mixture should be diverse and give a good impression.

The premises are much better if they are a good size, since every business that works well will run out of space. The microwave and a small grill are very useful, since the bar staff can serve the hot food seen in those display windows without leaving the bar. If not, they could have everything they need in order to make sandwiches on the spot. When it gets busier, one person in the kitchen will be able to make the sandwiches or whatever is ordered at the bar more quickly. You can get more staff for the bar or sales counter if necessary. The important things you need to achieve success: fast service, good quality and price. In these commercial sectors, you should be open and ready an hour before the other shops open and close an hour or more after they do. The amount of customers will quickly diminish when they close. Well, this isn't something definite since your business may continue selling but at a different pace.

SANDWICH SHOPS IN TOURIST AREAS. 72

Sometimes you see businesses of this type so small that it seems impossible that they could make money. But even though they're small, they often need plenty of staff to keep up with the demand. Some of them don't even have tables because of lack of space. They sell everything at theIt takes up a lot of time to sell the same thing. The aim of these businesses is to sell a lot in little time. If you're making very elaborate foods and you haven't prepared them in advance, the business won't work well enough. A good cook will resolve this problem efficiently, regardless of everything else. You could always have an à la carte restaurant, where the business, quality and price will be appropriate. In everything you make or sell, you must think like a mass producing factory, not like an artist. In the first case, you'll make money. In the second, you'll show off your skill and maybe get less profit. Of course, there is no rule without an exception.

WAITERS IN TOURIST AREAS. 73

The waiters' salary should be normal and include their insurance. Commission on sales is one way to improve money taken and allow the employees to increase their salary. If your employees are getting a good salary with commission, you won't be poor. If the salary of your employees is good but they don't earn commission, they'll work as if in an à la carte restaurant in which customer service is the most important thing.
 But they'll be less dynamic and sales will be reduced. When they're working quickly because the business needs it and the order is taken all at once, from the first dish to the coffee and dessert, this will be hugely beneficial to the business. The

service will be completed in little time.
The waiters will be taking away one plate and serving another, and the customer will already have finished before they know it. The tables will be free sooner and more customers can sit down.
This speed of service must never impact on good customer service. When they finish and are leaving, spend no more than ten or fifteen seconds in saying a warm goodbye, and maybe you'll see them again another day. Tourists are out of their environment and if one business treats them well, they'll be back. Taking the order all in one go. This is something which shows skill on the part of the waiter. At that moment, the customer wants to eat and order a lot of food, something which they won't do if you take an order after every course as if it were à la carte. If the full order isn't taken at the beginning, after they've eaten the first course, they won't be so hungry. That's why many restaurants don't sell either side orders or desserts.

PUBS WITH REGULARS. 74

In some pubs, regulars will come more and more often. It will usually be because they come to the area regularly, or it is near to their work or home. In these pubs, the owner has to be intelligent and welcome all customers equally. Don't become identified with any political party, for example. Some customers will gossip about you, your business and whatever they know about you. Stay neutral and you'll get a large customer base. Don't spread around your opinions. You're working - concentrate on that. All customers are good for you and you have to make them all smile. Otherwise, your business will go badly. You want it to go well, right? When they start talking about politics, go to another part of the pub and don't agree with disagree with their ideas.
The most common question you'll get from customers is

"What do you think?" Answer them, "I like playing football or going fishing. I'm not that interested in anything else". Be clever and carefully steer the conversation to another topic. In this way, you'll have all types of customers.

LOCAL PUBS. 75

Many customers are waiting for a pub to open so they can have a little drink, read the newspaper and whatever else. Don't fail them. There are often tapas in these pubs without going crazy. Some individually-wrapped pastries and other things you will have seen in these places. But some areas are so busy that the pubs are huge businesses and its features are among the best available. This is why I make a distinction between the different types of business in this trade.

The question of the sandwiches is something which will work in any of these businesses if the prices are competitive and you have the list of sandwiches in sight.

The grill and microwave allow you to serve customers without ever leaving the bar. If necessary, you could have a closed, glass-fronted fridge for the customers to see, where you can have cold meats, desserts, drinks, etc., a few tins of fish, tuna, clams, and whatever else. Remember to limit yourself to whatever you need. Whenever you serve a portion of food or some tapas with sauce, get used to putting a few wedges of bread on the plate for free. If you charge for them, they'll label you as stingy since you've marked it as a complementary tip for the business. Customers from these areas are more difficult. They are in their comfort area, so they can choose to keep coming back or not. Even if it's a small pub, cleanliness, good price and service are your weapons. Use them well.

TABLES IN OTHER PUBS. 76

It is an obligation to have tables in these pubs since many people drink while sitting down. A few read newspapers which you should have available for your customers. Have a range of newspapers - some politically left, others right. Don't worry about the cost. More than one customer will come in just to read the paper. Of course they have the obligation to buy something. If they read and don't buy anything, tell them clearly they are not in a public library. Remember that if you're not making profits, you're making losses. Have a few packs of cards for people to play. This will help attract people. Some places will allow them to play for money and for each game or round, the pub gets a share. In others, they charge for the table per hour. I would suggest you never allow illegal games. In these gaming tables, they will order drinks and pay at the end or whenever they want. You have to write down clearly what each person has. Don't trust your memory. You could also sell lottery tickets or tenths of them in the pub. In a board, write the winning lottery number or pools number every day, etc., etc. With these games, you'll attract more and more customers like addicts to your business. You can set up a pools ring to attract more long-term customers. You'll find things that customers need and want which you can loan to your customers. They are all good ways to get your customers to buy more.

THE CAFÉ TRADITION. 77

In these pubs, coffee is traditional. Make good coffee at a good price and you'll sell a lt. Don't think you won't make much money. The customers coming to your pub will make up for that. But no matter how much I tell you, every business is different. But anyway, I want to remind you how easy it is to attract customers. If you have space, you could have a pool table. Operators of gaming businesses may give you one for free, charge you a percentage or the full amount. You always have to be thinking about continuous development to see if it is something good for you. Coffee is very cheap, so you can sell alcohol cheap at the same time in order to stay competitive. Of course, you always have to make a profit. Pubs and their owners are not the sisters of charity.

PUBS IN COMMERCIAL AREAS OF CITIES. 78

Pubs in these areas work well as long as the people in charge are sensible and hard-working. These areas are where most customers are found. They go to these places because they know they'll find what they're looking for. You'll have customers coming in continuously if your prices are normal and the service is good. You should open an hour or more before the nearby shops open. The owners of these places are your first customers of the day. You should be there a little earlier to prepare what you need and get everything ready, whether it be pastries of the day, bread, etc.

The grill should be hot for making toast as should the coffee machine. You could do French toast with the bread from the day before (we'll talk about French toast later), Spanish omelettes and mini-sandwiches. As I said earlier, your few customers of the day may be the owners of shops nearby. You have to open your business ready to sell. Don't make excuses that you don't have pastries, the coffee machine is cold, or you don't have any omelettes to serve, because they'll walk out and not come back. They already had - before you opened the pub - somewhere else to have breakfast and they'll go back there. In some areas, you should open much earlier. Your mission is to get customers, taking them from competitors, and making them happy with good service. You can show these early-morning business owners quite a bit about running a business. They come to you because they want breakfast before opening their business and, if everything goes as planned, they'll get used to you and you'll have new regulars.

This influx of customers will continue all morning. There has to be someone in the kitchen making whatever is ordered, if necessary. Which came first, the chicken or the egg? That's the question. You can't wait until the customer orders something in order to find out what you want to sell. You have to plan what you want to sell and advertise it using price lists, menus and whatever else you come up with. Customers are always looking for something new. Exploit your intelligence and put into practice new ideas that you see or come up with. So there'll be more work? Of course. And more profits to take you where you want to be. This is different from working for someone else. The boss is the engineer of the ship, putting coal into the fire and going at the speed they want. Let me explain: innovation and offers are the responsibility of the boss since that's how to increase your workload. Who else would do it? An employee who would have to work more?

LUNCHTIME SERVICE. 79

Pubs that don't serve food at midday will lose customers and sales as people go out for lunch. You could have only a small menu with a few dishes and meals which your customers can have together with the coffee you offer. Throughout the afternoon you'll carry on selling and sales will be good while the shops are open. Two hours after the shops have closed, your sales will go down and you can tell if it's worth serving dinner. Every business needs to work more during the busy periods in their area. If you don't sell dinners, maybe others will. It's good to get up early and improve your service every day. Any pub, small as it may be, needs to serve some food at midday so that the sales are increased for the day.

PROFITS THROUGH FOOD. 80

Here's something you should always remember: "take lots of money every day". When you start serving food, you can see if there is a future in it. What a customer spends on food in half an hour might be the same that four or five might spend in the same time. 50% or more of the money taken in a day at the counter with three staff can be very similar to the money taken by the same people during lunchtime. If you have twelve or fourteen tables and you use them for food, sales will go up between 30 and 50% each day, and they'll keep going up. That's the difference with serving food. This experience can open new horizons to the restaurant business if you've never done that before. Most of your money and profits come from food.

THE COST OF A POPULAR MENU. 81

Setting good prices on your menu depends on the products that you use. Let's suppose a starter of vegetables or pasta. The first thing you have to know is the price of each ingredient for each meal. A kilo of peas is enough for ten plates if you add enough other vegetables and condiments. The total cost of this portion of peas ready to serve is not more than double the cost of the dried peas you bought. If you add vegetables, pasta, rice or potatoes, it'll be even cheaper.

You could also sell macaroni, spaghetti or any other pasta. These are the cheapest types. A plate of pasta with tomato and cheese could cost less than half the price of the peas. Don't forget about paella with rice - if it is done well - or white rice with fried eggs. These dishes are well-liked by customers while being very profitable for your business.

<u>Main courses.</u> I can't teach you how to cook here, but I can make you understand that being an entrepreneur is the best way to make money. Combination platters generally include things like eggs, pork, medium-priced veal, chicken and fish, not too expensive. Of course we're talking about popular food here. Garnishes for some of these combination platters mustn't be complicated. You can add salted vegetables, mashed potato, white rice, and many other low-cost dishes which a professional chef could have ready to heat up when required. Desserts and side dishes are important for giving a good service and increasing money taken.

STARTING A BUSINESS OF DIRECT SALE TO THE PUBLIC. 82

In any business which sells directly to the public, when you first start, customers will come in comparing quality and prices with other pubs they went to before you were there. Remember that allies and arrangements with other people in the same trade and area will hurt your business. Your friendship with competitors could stop you setting prices freely. Lower your prices of coffee a certain % below your competitors' prices. Good coffee contains ten grams of grains plus sugar, then add the electricity. You can check the price by dividing the price of a kilo of coffee by 100.
Double it for good coffee and that will be your total price including other costs. The price of quality coffee and good service can be your Trojan horse to get good customers. The competition won't like you lowering your prices because they already have their tradition and customers, but you can still

beat them. If you can't make a payment one day, don't think they'll pay it for you. You have to do what is best for you. If you fight and you are competitive, you will win. If you do what your competitors do, you'll lose. If you want to make friends with your competitors, you'll end up agreeing to fixed prices, you'll be coerced and won't have freedom to fight. You have to be aggressive in order to grow. If you fix your income and profits and don't take the path of aggressiveness, like a good competitor, you'll never get the best out of any business or product that falls into your hands. If you follow these methods, you can be sure you'll get to where you want to be

You mustn't forget that you're the person in charge of your business and that your customers come to you because of what you do. Don't let others take the reins from you. Whatever you do should have your mark of originality. Don't let anyone snatch it from you. You'll find the path to luck if you're clever. Remember that one person alone doesn't have time to make money. Even so, don't let anyone in on your act or your secrets to success. Selling a lot for little is much better than selling a little for a lot.

CAN I OPEN A BUSINESS SELLING GLASSES OF WINE? 83

Anything can be the focus for your business if you study it well enough. Many pubs are afraid of alcoholics who swarm like flies to a pub that sells wine at a good price. It all depends on how you organise yourself and at what price you sell it. A friend of mine prepared a freezer exclusive to have chilled glasses ready to serve to customers. When they asked for a wine, he asked them: "Cold?" If they wanted it cold, he'd give it to them in a chilled glass with wine from the fridge. When he first served wine or any other drink in a chilled glass to customers, you could see the look of admiration in their face. Then they got used to it and brought their friends. These glasses could also be used to serve other drinks. He even served some kinds of bar snack, like olives, for free (or included in the price) with the wine. He never sold wine cheaper than mid-range beer. It was a good wine among other standard ones.

Study the price of whatever you buy. If you work intelligently in everything you do, you'll have made a giant step forward. Don't forget the ideas that come from your head are the ones that make you successful. People that are truly successful send 10% of their time with physical work and 90% thinking. Even though nothing is ever definite when it comes to percentages, we have to remember that it's all a question of using our intelligence and intuition. You earn money by being clever and leave the physical work to others..

 Or do it yourself until you need other employees. Here's an observation on customers. These days, most customers who go to pubs have almost everything they need at home. They go to pubs for simple reasons, some because of tradition or momentum, to get into the business, meet someone or play slot machines while they have a drink. It's important that they come in and much more important that they come back. If they come back, they let you know that your business is worth it. A friendly greeting to every customer that comes in can help them relax and make them feel at home. If you ignore them when they come in, many of them won't come back. Every human being needs respect and friendliness.

METHODS FOR GETTING CUSTOMERS. 84

When you start opening a business of this type, it's a good idea to send out a few invitations saying: "Come and have a coffee on the house." Or whatever else. You can give out this invitation to businesses and homes near to your premises, as long as they are not catering businesses. This will get people to know about your business that wouldn't come along if it weren't for the invitation. They already have their favourite place where they drink coffee or whatever. If you have good quality and low prices, you're doing a good job or keeping them coming back. Lower the prices of your coffee and most popular beer with respect to your competitors. They'll be left without customers while you're earning your living. Advertise your business with any means possible so that people get to know your business "exists".Giving your customers drinks on the house will get you "regulars". For example, you can give people that come in a few times their drinks or food for free because it's your birthday or someone else's: "Today it's my birthday, or my son's or my wife's, so it's on the house". Oryou prepare a certain drink, like a few jars of sangria for free. (Don't worry.

I know that nobody ever became rich giving away things for free.) Think of this as giving water to a rosebush so that it gives you magnificent roses. If you do the same every year, you'll get more clients and more money.

They'll thank you for your generosity every time they come to drink your coffee. Remember that coffee costs you. Every business does the same. You have to be ambitious without being selfish or stingy. That's part of the publicity you need to grow. Invent a "customer day". Remember that everything you do will be good for publicity. Do you think that Coca-Cola, after a hundred years in the world market, needs publicity? Of course, because they want everything in the world to have one in their fridge so that every family drinks it and nobody forgets them. That's why they spend so much on advertising.

OTHER GOOD THINGS TO SELL A PUB. 85

You can also sell other things in your pub, not because you'll earn a lot of money but because it's better customer service. You could have aspirin, lighters, pools tickets and coupons, individual bags of snacks, such as almonds, hazelnuts, peanuts, tins of sardines, chocolate bars, etc. Some customers will get used to taking something home for their kids or that they come along one day. Time is a great teacher and you'll get to know what customers want, within reason. Some of these items may not make a profit but, as a consequence, you'll sell a lot more. Never look a gift horse in the mouth.

YOUR STAFF'S GOOD CUSTOMER SERVICE. 86

Having staff with good personalities is essential for your business to succeed. They can be more or less attractive but they must be polite, neat and friendly with the customers. People who are not like this are terrible staff since they scare away customers. Since we want to succeed, we need the best workers possible. A customer can live without going to a pub, but a pub can't live without customers.

GENERALISING INCENTIVES NEVER GIVES GOOD RESULTS. 87

In some business sectors, they may be extra benefits besides commission. You must do the calculations and know when and who to give these benefits to, since generalising never gives good results. There are good workers who are efficient even without getting any benefits.
There are others who have a good salary but have to be encouraged and not let out of your sight, making sure they have enough to do.

There are people who, if you reward them without explanation, might think that the business does it because it's suitable for them, or they are making a lot of money. Those that are rewarded without explanation will take it as their right which will later be difficult to rectify job..

PREVIOUS JOBS, 88

Many entrepreneurs without a job start thinking they could start working for themselves while looking for another job. In such cases, they don't have the slightest idea that in doing other jobs which you've never thought about before, they start opening other doors which, in time, will make them into businessmen.

When this restlessness is awakened, it's the most important moment of their life. Something is activated in their brain and they start acting according to their thoughts. It's common that experience from previous jobs, posts or trades will help the future entrepreneur as a base for starting their own first business. In this book, you'll discover that luck is with you, and that you'll find the starting point in catering or any other profession, even if you've never done it before.

CHAPTER 3   89

OPENING A CAFÉ.   **90**

There are different types of cafés which we will now summarise. Some are luxurious for a certain class of people, while others are more functional, designed for anyone. All catering businesses have a defined class. You can open one and try to give it the category you want. All cafés have their cups and restaurants their forks, but the technicians from the appropriate official department will be the ones who make the final decision on your category after having checked your building and services. Many catering businesses are in a category lower than the service they offer, something which is not possible in reverse.

UPPER-CLASS CATERING BUSINESSES. 91

In these companies, all food prepared and consumed by the customers has to be of the best quality. Its facilities will relate to each other. The prices and level of service are higher than those of a normal café, since its competition is based on being the best at everything. The price won't matter up to a certain point since the demand only the best. Top-class cafés must be run by fully-trained and experienced professionals. These are special businesses which require a large investment. You can't and mustn't run unnecessary risks, by giving these tasks to people who don't know the trade very well. They have to be recognised, responsible professionals.
Entrepreneurs who start this type of business and have the money don't necessarily need to be professionals. You can find good specialised catering managers in the market. Investors who want to properly run their business have to fully integrate themselves into it, knowing what every

employee has to do, participating in or running the administration of the business, and in only a little time, they'll know how the business works. Their direct participation is completely essential for the business to be correctly financed. Remember: the owner needs to either run a business well or sell it. It's a good saying which can work well with the help of the entrepreneur and the collaboration or an expert, either as an employee or a partner.

OPENING A NORMAL CAFÉ.   92

If you want to open a café and you've never worked in the trade before, look for an ideal professional to help you start it up. Even if you have no experience of the trade, after reading this book, you won't notice so much. This professional you get to help you must be involved even from buying the furniture, equipment, etc. Give them a contract for however long necessary and with his collaboration and your help, it'll work well from day one. You don't need any type of temporary association. Look for professionals who aren't much older than you but have recognised professional responsibility, since catering is based on being constantly dynamic. In only a little time, the entrepreneur, being a person who remembers everything they see, will have learned enough to start taking over skilfully from this professional. Even so, don't rush to get rid of people you still need. One person "working" alone is not a business. It is a robot to works only to get enough to survive.

Catering needs enough hands to get good service. Always remember it's a business and you need to create jobs. When you start a small business, you can start with minimal staff but, after some time, it won't grow if there isn't enough work to give to employees so that you can say: "I have a business that produces".

WHEN WILL IT START MAKING ME MONEY? 93

All in good time. At first, everything will be costs. If you have a good location, sales will rise and you'll soon see profits. We've already done a few calculations on costs and sales. If we make a sales plan in a new business and we don't know how it's going to turn out, we'll only have the doubt of whether to get new employees before or after being sure. You have to start on the first day with enough hands to work.

After you see it working, you'll know whether you have too many staff or not enough.

As a minimum, in the first two weeks, you need enough staff otherwise you'll look ridiculous in front of your future customers. In this trial period, you'll know if the business could do with more staff or less. Potential customers will be waiting for new businesses to open and your first impression has to be the best. Even if you don't make any profits, it doesn't matter. The customers that sit down might look like they are in no hurry but serve them quickly or they'll walk out without buying anything. The same goes for those at the bar.

Your staff must be waiting for the customers to say what they want so they can be served quickly. They don't mind spending time waiting in a pub or café but only after they've been served, not before. The entrepreneur has to worry that their business will work, that their services or products are selling at not only the best price but with the best quality, speed and customer service... Everything can be learned about work. There are jobs and trades that, when you learnthem, you realise that they are routines and that you have to do them to learn and understand them.

POPULAR CAFÉ . 94

They are aimed at a large percentage of the population. The difference between them is the location, investment, size of the premises and, to some extent, the choice of customer you're aiming the business at, though this is all relative.
Customers decide for themselves if they like a business, so the service, quality and price have to be appropriate with the place. There's no point opening any old business with bad service and quality, and prices similar to other better ones with better services in general. For these businesses to work, they have to be functional and modern, without luxuries. Good, young, efficient and clean staff that clean up well. You need to have enough space. Competition is based on: quality, service, and fair prices. In this book, you'll find other catering chapters which you should read and compare with this to draw your own conclusions.

TRADES WHICH ARE NEW TO YOU. 95

You've never worked in catering before? If you haven't, don't worry too much - just enough! Many entrepreneurs who have never done something before commit to opening a business. Through hard, consistent work, they end up being competent professionals. Let's imagine that you want to start a business of this type. First you need to find a place where you want to set up. A particular site will not be suitable for all business types.

 The ideal premises will be large and with enough space for pedestrians in front. Your rental contract should be for an indefinite time, or at least for 15 or 20 years, or even more. Hold on. Before signing the buying or rental contract, look for a technical architect who can go with you to see it, so that you can together enquire in the town hall or appropriate department if there would be any problem in opening your business there. If the answer is positive, you can get your lawyer to draw up, modify or negotiate a contract convenient for you which you can present to the owner of the premises.

GENERAL LAYOUT. 96

The technician will draw up a draft plan in which you can discuss the layout, and suggest ideas that you think are necessary (this draft is so that you can get a good idea of what you want), or change whatever is necessary, before being completed. After the plan is completed, have another look, and then present it at the appropriate office for approval. You have to bear municipal laws on mind because if you present a plan for approval and you haven't respected the rules, it's possible that it will be rejected. The technical architect is the best person to do this as he will know the laws and be able to resolve any doubts.

EXAMPLE OF THE LAYOUT OF PREMISES WITH A SIZE OF 200 M2. 97

Let's give an example of premises which are 200 m2 in size. The most important areas are the public area, the kitchen and the bathrooms. Distribution of space: bar and public area, 125 m2; kitchen, 15 m2; ladies toilets. 8 m2... Gents toilets, 8m2; toilets and changing rooms for employees, 8 m2 for ladies and 8 for men; storeroom 10 m2; office, 8 m2; other corridors, 8 to 12 m2... These are approximate sizes with the intention that it be a good place for customers to be. The size of the toilets can be made larger or small according to the technician's criteria. Money is made in the public area and the kitchen, where the food is prepared. Ifwe have fewer square metres available, we have to adapt to what we have. The technician has the final word on what the law allows or prohibits.

SSENTIALS. 98

Some things in catering are essential and can't be left out of the plan, such as the extractor fan, emergency exit, amount of space legislated for each area, and these are related to the premises itself, such as the size of the kitchen, the drains and not much else. Complying with these rules is important so that your business will be able to open. The architect is the one who must have final say on the layout of certain general things. Work equipment and decor is not obligatory and so the owner has the choice of where they go.

The owner can suggest modifications after getting different opinions from specialist technicians in catering or whatever type of business it is and from those that are fitting out the business. An example: the technician prepares a plan with a certain width for the counter of the bar, the location of shelves, and so on, which the owner can alter, since they are put as suggestions in these plans. In the distribution plans, only the large installations are essential though others may be drawn in. What this means is that whatever is not fixed can be changed by the person paying to fit in with their working methods. The work itself can be done by the businessman himself or the company that he feels convenient.

When the plan is complete, after the owner's modifications and suggestions, the plan will be presented by the technician in the college of architects to be looked at. After a few days, you'll be contacted and told you can go to the college to pay for the project, including the technicians fees. You've already paid the architect, whether you go through with it or not. No refunds.

THE BAR OR COUNTER. 99

The counter should fit as many customers as possible at one time along it. A bar is the best way to do this, according to the plans. When you plan the layout of a pub or café counter, remember that, if there is only one member of staff and many customers at the same time, the worker has to be able to serve and charge efficiently. If the pub is large, you could try a U-shaped bar, connected by the open part of that U to the kitchen. However you lay it out, it should be connected to the kitchen so that the supplies come out easily and quickly.

The suggestion of the U form is to make service easier, being near to the customers, the fridges, the coffee machine and everything else necessary. The shelves and coffee machine must be in the centre of the space left by the U, and the work areas under the counter or below the centre. According to the business, you might choose to have a small bar with mostly tables, so that the customers can take their orders back with them once they've paid. This way of working is positive and often used because you don't need to be waiting for the customer to pay.

If you have service with waiters, you need more staff. It's all related to the class of business. You'll have better service and higher prices, or vice versa. The exit from the bar to serve tables must be at one end of the bar to cause minimum bother to customers where there will be a space reserved for the waiters. You could have a few bar stools but not too many. Leave space for standing customers. When starting, a bar stool every two metres of the bar should be enough. If you see that you need more, you can put a couple more.

SIZE OF THE BAR. 100

The height could be around 1.15 and 1.2 m from the ground, and the width around 50 or 55 cm. These are approximate measures since the entrepreneur will decide the height and width after seeing many other bars in other places. The interior part of the bar. At hand height (about 80 cm from the ground), there will be work counters, a sink and rack for glasses, bottle fridges, drinks and many other things. Bottle racks which open at the top are quicker for service and use of space. Those that open from the front are not so useful as their interior space is not used so well, but you can use the top for a work area, for storing glasses, dishes or other equipment. The most practical for large amounts of sales are those that open at the top. In a banquet, for example, we can wear a bow tie and leather shoes, but if we want to go to "war", you need light, well-tied boots to serve thousands of customers in little time.

DISPLAY WINDOWS IN THE BAR. 101

All food shown to the public needs to be shielded from the air, from customers' food. It shouldn't be touched. This food is usually held in refrigerated windows, with the part facing the customer closed and with a door facing the waiter that can be opened. They usually take up 50% of the width of the bar, with the rest of it used by customers. Customers have these displays right in front of their eyes and some will not be able to resist the snacks and tapas inside. As well as keeping food cold, these displays also act as publicity. Both the windows and the food within needs to always be sparkling. The windows have to be cleaned every day. Take out the contents and clean inside and out. It's part of advertising your food, which will sell as well as it is presented.

WHY DON'T SOME BUSINESSES HAVE DISPLAY WINDOWS? 102

The owner knows that, by using displays, they have control over health matters and what customers eat. Some municipalities will demand it of some places. Other areas don't have them for whatever reason. It all depends on the focus of the business and the customers you want to attract. If a bar doesn't have these windows, the customers will grab tapas and eat them.
The bartender will ask them what they ate. He'll charge them based on what they say. It's an act of trust. It works like that because there are more sales and more chance for customers to eat more and pay less. The owner knows that some people will take advantage, but while there are so many sales, it is convenient. It's a psychological act, that you can watch them and they can eat freely.Contents of display windows. Some will be ready to eat; others are prepared to be heated in the microwave when ordered. Other windows might have sweet or savoury pastries, cold meats, etc. The temperature can be set appropriately. These will be sold as we go along, but the cheapest and most practical are usually the mass produced ones.

DISHWASHER AT THE BAR. 103

It may be small for staying at the bar and washing at the same time as serving where there are relatively few people. The sink can be used whenever there are very few people and sales are slow. If you have a busier business, glasses can go to the kitchen or whatever is the best place, where you can put a larger industrial dishwasher. When working, used glasses goin the dishwasher which you have in the work counter, and once full, you start it up straight away. This isn't the same in all cafés. It has to depend on the amount of space available, staff and customers.

DRAUGHT BEER. 104

If we install draught beer on tap, we'll have to decide where to put it on the bar for best service. This will become the centre of the bar. Underneath the bar, there'll be a space reserved for at least two barrels. You can have more in other places if necessary, and another space for the compressor (which makes the beer cold). You can have a small door near the barrels to facilitate getting them inside. The brand beer companies will take responsibility for installing and repairing the pumps completely free.
 The beer manufacturers will compete to install their brand of beer and the taps in larger businesses. It's a custom that when a new business opens in which they think a lot of beer will be sold (because it has a good location), they will give you the first twenty or thirty barrels for free.
The manufacturers therefore get more customers through your business selling that brand of beer. The taps are made with their brand and it wouldn't be correct to sell the wrong brand of beer through a tap. You might get offers from soft drinks through taps, like colas or juices. They are also installed and repaired at the cost of the company that provides them.
When you sell a box of beer or other drinks, we know what we're earning. When we sell from barrels manufactured by others, we have to trust them and their beer. Every person has their own opinion. A box of cola syrup can produce two hundred drinks, once the soda water is automatically added to fill a glass. The concentration of the syrup is set by the company. You won't know how many glasses you'll get out of them because there is no meter. As you can see, it's a question of trust. There are many bottled drinks and they also

sometimes break.

INSTALLING A BEER ON TAP. 105

When you do the bar plan, you have to figure in the installation of the beer tap. If you want this, you should phone the most popular beer company (the one that sells the most) and tell the sales manager to come to your business. When he comes, tell him that another brand (which is their competitor) is offering you free barrels of beer: Tell him that if they put the tap and beer in, you thought that if they could make a better offer, you'll accept it. Now you should stop talking. This sales guy will tell you that you should put his beer in, and so on and so forth. He may ask you how many barrels they'll give you. Just tell him "a lot" and that you'll study the better offer. This is called negotiating with an ace up your sleeve. As well as these barrels, you can also ask him for awning for the front of your business if you need it, tables and chairs for a terrace or for inside, umbrellas for tables, cups, glasses, coasters, napkins, etc.
These companies have an advertising department and this will all come from there. It's crucial to get as much out of them as you can for free. It's not blackmail, even if it looks like it. It's strong negotiation which we can't just ignore. Don't accept the first offer they make you. You might get something extra.

THE COFFEE MACHINE. 106

You'll need a space of around a metre or a metre and a half for the coffee machine and grinder. It all depends on its size. You can buy them in groups of two or four but you should buy whatever is most convenient. In some businesses, you only see one large one. In others, you might have more than one, such as important tourist areas, cafés and truck-stops, or other large, busy businesses.

A business which serves a lot of coffee needs the appropriate machinery. In cafés, the customer wants it straight away. It's about quick service. If it's a large building, two medium-sized coffee machines should be about right.

CONSUMPTION OF COFFEE. 107

According to the place in which the business is located, it may be necessary to get a better team of coffee machines. When many people enter at the same because some coaches have stopped outside, as can happen in roadside pubs or restaurants, thirty or more people could be asking for coffee at the same time. Coffee is something which sells a lot at affordable prices. It's best to sell at a reduced cost. You use 10 grams of coffee in a good cup, as we've said before. In tourist areas as we've mentioned, there is no competition and the prices are usually good for the industry.

COFFEE GRINDER. 108

This has a dispenser which limits the amount of coffee you want to put in. You put coffee granules in the grinder which grinds them up according to what you need. The fact that it makes a little at a time causes the room to smell of coffee which is good for making more coffee addicts. It should be next to the coffee machine. A good location for the two of them together will be at the back of the serving staff when they are facing the customer. They like to see how the coffee falls into the cup. The coffee machine has a vaporiser which is used to heat liquids, make chocolate espresso and infusions. It also has a tap for hot water for anything else you need it for, such as infusions. Coffee cups are usually on top of the coffee machine where they are kept warm and retain the smell of the coffee when used.

IMPORTANT COFFEE MACHINES.   109

Inside they have a water inlet connecting it to the main supply. When it is opened, water enters which is then used to make the coffee... The water container shows you the level of water inside which you have to keep an eye on so it doesn't stay empty. When you let water in, don't leave it open to go and do something else. If you forget and it fills up too much, you'll have to take some out so the vapour pressure is correct and the coffee machine doesn't overheat. Until it returns back to its normal temperature and pressure, which may take a while, many people will walk away without coffee and some may not come back.

When water is going in, you have to watch it so it doesn't fill up completely and lose its pressure. When you're filling it with water and something comes up and you have to go away from the coffee machine, close the inlet and fill it up later. It's a good idea to have two coffee machines, because if one stops working, you'll never have to say no to a customer. In places where sometimes the water gets cut off, it's common to have a large tank of water in a high place when there is no water from the main supply. It's also worth putting water in the coffee machine from there when the water from the main supply isn't

offered at a good price, they are charged extra. Good prices on toast and certain pastries can be very successful and earn a lot of profit and reputation. Whatever we make will always be more profitable than what we buy ready-made. The public wants good, big and cheap. If they are served elegantly and skilfully, even the most demanding customers will ask for them. Although competitively priced, never underestimate the value of these sales when it comes to profits. It's like serving good food with some kind of tablecloth. The price will be cheaper depending on the type you use but the quality can be the same. The aim has to be that customer notice the difference when comparing it to other businesses

Commerce has to be a continuous struggle, not only to sell enough but to sell more every day. Large or small businesses compete with their products to get people to want to buy them. Nearby businesses are used to getting good profits on work they are doing, and they won't be happy about new competitors appearing. They will go on with their same prices and services, and when they realise, we'll have a business that a percentage of their customers will have chosen as better.

When this work is planned and completed in terms of mass production, it's not necessary to be an expert in catering, since it becomes a routine job. Once you've learned these business systems, the second will work perfectly. The first is always the most difficult. If a business works well, whatever it is, don't think about it too much. Open another in a good location. That's how chains start. When you decide to duplicate the business in another place, you already have the experience and staff who are used to your ideas. We have to make sure that every business we open works on our ideas, being personally inside the business as long as necessary, until it works correctly under the charge of a supervisor.

OPENING A CAFÉ IN THE MORNING. 110

When the business is opened in the morning, the coffee machine mustn't be cold. When it closes at the end of the day, clean everything, fill the coffee machine with water, don't unplug it and it will stay warm during the night. The thermostat will keep it warm with little power consumption, like a domestic water heater. If you open your business, plug in the coffee machine and say to the customers that come in asking for coffee: "Sorry, sir, the coffee machine is cold!", you might say it politely but you're hurting the business more than you think. It will be a tragedy for the business. Customers will turn around and leave and you won't see them again. Every day you'll lose more customers. If you do what I say, you'll get more customers every day. And with the profits you make from those first few coffees sold in the morning, you will cover the electricity you spent during the night. So that the coffee machine works well: From opening when there are many people coming in, the kitchen has to be at the service of the person at the counter. The staff working in the kitchen have as their mission, as well as preparing food to serve throughout the day, to make as quickly and as carefully as possible whatever the counter staff ask for. The service has to be so dynamic so that the customers wait as little time as possible. Customers in the morning won't want to speak to you to say good morning or chat. They're going to or coming from work and what they need is fast and efficient service. If there is no-one in the kitchen in the morning, that's why you have the grill and microwave. You have to take advantage of your intelligence.

At midday or other food times, you will be serving, meals, combination platters, tapas, portions of good, sandwiches and so on. When starting, if the business is still small, you can have just a small menu of two starters and two main courses, to choose one from each group at a price suitable for the company. The quicker you serve and the customer consumes, the more profitable these combinatio platters are for the business. How do you make combination platters? You'll know soon. You'll read about it later in this book. Whatever you make, prepare and sell will give you more profits. "If you don't know how to smile, don't start a business to sell directly to customers." Like everything else, the seller has to learn to smile. If he wants to sell, he has to be like an actor and play that role. A large portion of your success will come from that. Success will depend partially on the person who runs the kitchen. They have to know how to cook and make tapas (with experience of working in a pub or restaurant). I suggest that, if you have a small business, you have a woman in the kitchen because when she finishes working, she'll leave it clean and tidy. This is something you can state when hiring her.

STAFF WORKING HOURS. 111

If the business is open all day, the ideal thing is to have two shifts even with minimal staff. The first shift starts first thing in the morning and ends when lunch service finishes. The second starts before serving food to the public and ends at the end of the day. It's common that waiters eat in the business when they work during meal times. The second shift starts at twelve or twelve thirty (if they eat in the business), they eat and immediately relieve those on the first shift so that they can eat. They can also eat elsewhere and come to work when they are due to start.
In catering, staff should be given their meals on the house. If you don't give them their meals, they'll eat what they want when you can't see them and it'll end up more expensive anyway. You can't work with food and not eat it. You can also have a rota which changes each week so that everyone can have a day off through the week.

Each week, write the shifts on a piece of paper and put it up for staff to see without favouring anybody on any particular day. Everyone should have mornings or afternoons free whenever it is their turn. If the business doesn't close any day of the week, you'll have an extra employee so that each one can have a day off during the week. Favouritism with a certain employee will cause hard feelings with the rest. To stay in control, the businessman has to be fair and equal, generating a good working environment with his staff and the business. After you read this, you, as an entrepreneur, will renew and improve my ideas.

POPULAR CAFÉ. 112

A café can be modest to a certain extent, but it is essential to have one person in the kitchen who knows very well what they are doing. This is basic for the business to run well. Some services can be completed at the counter while work is slow. Kitchen staff will always have something to prepare. Combination platters are quick to serve but need to be prepared ahead of time. They aren't improvised at the moment they are ordered. These meals have to be half-prepared, and then finished and served at the moment they are ordered. You can always fully prepare a few set meals, though only a few to see how they go. Note: Before setting up a café or other catering business, it's a good idea to go to a big city and eat in some popular central cafés or restaurants. You should take a camera to take photos of whatever you can.
These trips may be very instructive for you. You'll see an infinity of meals, sales systems and layouts which will give you further ideas. You must also know that, although I mention some things about the kitchen, I won't teach you to cook. This book has been written to show you how to organise a business to sell a lot. We will leave the kitchen to the professionals. However, if you've never worked in the trade before, what I explain here will help you have an idea, since the first step is to get a professional. I want to convince you that you make money by using your head. People who are organised and clever can get to wherever they want, and you can be one of them.

COMBINATION PLATTERS AND OTHER MEALS. 113

From combination platters and set meals, you can expect to get more than 60% of your daily income. How these are composed is not something set in stone. Every business invents their own, or copies from other businesses or cookery books. To a certain extent, both the cook and entrepreneur should work together, since the entrepreneur sees the business side of things and the cook only thinks about how the food looks and is made. You can make as many different meals as you want. Practically, it should be between eight and twelve, which is enough to offer food to different customers. You can take photos for advertising at the front door, and the same photos in a smaller size for the menu given to the customer. This might seem very expensive but it is something important for quick and efficient sales. Photos of each dish should be numbered to avoid mistakes and make work quicker. If you put a photo of every number on the wall of the kitchen, the cooks will work quicker and more efficiently since they want have to ask anything to make the food as it should be.

IDEAS FOR A COMBINATION PLATTER. 114

Example of a dish: You can make a meal with a grilled steak, salted green beans, white rice or slices of tomato. Others could come with some kind of side which a good cook could make cheaply. White rice can be boiled, drained and stored in a fridge to be reheated for each portion, while the meat can be cut into a steak, kept in the fridge and ready to be grilled. The green beans are boiled and prepared to give an extra touch of heat, and the slices of tomato can be cut there and then.
Boiled eggs with the shell removed can be kept in the fridge.

When the kitchen gets the order for a dish, put the meat or fish on the grill and, while it is cooking, prepare the rest.

The base food in any meal can be fish, pork, beef, chicken or cold meats. This can be accompanied with white rice which you can reheat, croquettes ready to be fried, plain omelettes ready to be done, fried eggs, tins of asparagus in the fridge, tins of peppers ready to fry, slices of normal and Parma ham, and other cold meats cut and in the fridge, a block of cheese ready for cutting, some lettuce, mashed potato made in advance or when ordered, and served hot. Grilled chickens ready to be cut into quarters or halves and sold with a side dish which could be chips. These have to be half-fried, only needing to be fried briefly when it's time to serve it. Etc., etc... and we could go on.

All of these food items can be either prepared in advanced, half-prepared or ready to prepare. You always have to use food that won't go off. Even if you're not very familiar with the catering business, you won't be a total novice now. It would be a mistake to start a business like this without having a good cook. He would take care of the issue of cooking and help the boss keep his head above the water.

We also have another good ally on our side: freezing. If we take full advantage of this, we'll never throw anything away. You don't have to prepare everything I mentioned above for your business. After seeing other in different cafés, you'll know what is best for you. You can make many dishes in little time if all the food you need on that day is prepared in advance. If you are making fried food, you can have them ready to be fried. The dishes that take longest to make are the first ones. Once they are ready, the whole dish is ready.

My participation isn't as a cook. It is as an adviser on how to make money. This paragraph is to clear things up for the entrepreneur. The other, about the kitchen, is more for the cook with the essential help of the entrepreneurs in all things, small and large.

The cook is the technician is preparing the food. The entrepreneur is the economist who decides the prices. The amount of food on each plate is decided in collaboration between the two.

DESSERT AND COFFEE MENU. 115

These can be together on one menu or separate. If they haven't ordered dessert when the order was first taken, when you see that they are finishing, before taking away their plates, without asking them if they want dessert, put the dessert menu into the hands of the customer.

Then, take away the plates and come back with the order book, or <u>you can take the order immediately</u> and then take away the plates. What are we aiming at here? Not to lose the chance to take the orders as soon as possible. Take the order for desserts and coffee or other drinks at the same time.

Time is important and so are sales. The mission of the staff member has to be to take the order without delay. In catering, taking the order should be done as quickly as possible. If you let the customers think how much the dessert costs, sometimes they'll decide they don't want any. You have to make sure they don't think too much in this case. We're not trying to cheat the customers here, just to get them to buy more. With desserts, a good salesman can increase the daily income by 15% or more. Once the order has been taken, take away the menu then and there, so that they don't decide to change their minds since their choice might already be ready..

PHOTOS OF COMBINED PLATTERS. 116

You should find a professional photographer to take your photos as they will come out much better. Take copies of them since they will fade with time, so you can take them down and put up new ones. Some businesses have photos so old and faded that it is embarrassing for them. You can also take photos of ice-cream or other desserts that you want to sell as specialities.

There are catering supply companies who have photos of combination platters, desserts, sandwiches and so on which they can supply, but they'll always be the same as in other companies. If you want your business to be different, make your own. Photos of dishes and other foods are good at selling themselves, and if they are placed on view of passers-by, all the better.

TAKING THE ORDER. 117

This is a task which must be done quickly and cleverly. In only a few seconds, the customer can change their opinion and not order any sides, desserts, etc. It's a good idea to give commission to waiters as a group so they work as a team. Commission is a diverse topic and depends on the businessman, his point of view of the business and of the trade. Regardless, you can be sure that sales will easily increase with this formula. Commission on sales for the staff who make the sales is vital for increasing the increasing the amount ordered.

COST AND SALE PRICES ON COMBINATION PLATTERS. 118

As with everything else done in the business, the sales prices are decided by the owner. To calculate the price, add the cost of the products on the plate and multiply by three or maybe more. This could be your sales price, though you could also reduce it. There is no fixed rule. The entrepreneur has to know the cost of what they buy and the amount of dishes he can get from a kilo of fruit or meat, or the amount of cups or glasses that you get from each bottle. You must know the cost price of every product used, and soon you'll be an expert. When you work out the value of combined platters, you have to be alert. If the person who makes the calculations of the sales prices is not the owner, they may make them less competitive which reduces the number of customers. The entrepreneur has to do these in order to make sure more customers come every day. The amount of customers can be reduced by staff who don't want to work so much. They'll sell less and be more comfortable at work. You'll have to buy stools for them to sit down and rest on soon. Do you understand what you have to do? You have to keep these things in mind.

BREAD, DRINKS AND DESSERTS. 119

The customer has to pay for every item they order unless we offer a menu with everything or some things included. A good sales person (waiter) with drinks, desserts and other extras, can double the money taken. A slow waiter taking orders will lead us to ruin. Not just anyone can take orders. To do it well, you need skill and psychology. To increase the sales, there is only the matter of a few seconds and you need to rely on your waiter's skill.

KITCHENS IN CAFÉS. 120

If customer service is a café is important, the kitchen and supervisor are no less so. If the kitchen isn't working well, the business in general won't either. The kitchen has to be equipped with the necessary tools to work quickly. An extractor fan is essential which should be installed before buying or renting the premises in the first place. If there isn't an extractor fan, you'll have to make sure the contract you sign includes the authorisation to install one.

The technician will be able to tell you if and where you can put it. If it's possible to install a vent, it has to be clear in the contract. (That the tenant is authorised to install a vent or extractor fan wherever is most convenient) or however a lawyer might express it.

KITCHEN EQUIPMENT. 121

A dishwasher, slicing machine, whisk, waste disposal unit, a double sink, solid shelves for plates and cutlery, other shelves, a cooker with various hobs, oven, hot water boiler, Express pans, work counters, casserole dishes, frying pans and others, a good industrial fridge-freezer, and other necessary items, a space for the bin, etc. We are talking about the basics here. There are others which may or may not be necessary. Anything you need will be found in specialised industry shops. They can help you with the types of dishes and equipment, tables, chairs and other café, pub, restaurant etc. furniture you might need. Be careful - if they see money coming, they'll sell you things you don't need. Drinks suppliers, when you open a business, will give you cups, glasses, chairs, tables, awning, signs, etc. for free. Everything they give you will have their brand or logo on it. If your business isn't upper-class, take them as long as they are free. If your business is in a place with a lot of foot traffic, you'll get more from them since it is free publicity for them.

VENTILATION FOR YOUR PREMISES.   122

We've already talked about the kitchen. You can also think about air conditioning, both hot and cold, or even a simple window looking out into the patio or garden can be enough for air to come through, maybe even forced through by a fan.

You have to make sure that the smoke doesn't exit through the door of your business which could cause unexpected problems with your neighbours. Make sure it is only air coming out. If your business is going well, take care of your neighbours. There'll always be one that doesn't like what you do and wants to cause you problems. When you open the business, invite your neighbours to have a drink. It all depends on your generosity. If you do this, maybe they won't try to mess with you so much for every little thing. Certainly the other neighbours won't pay them any attention. Don't give them the chance to make claims against you. Many people don't sleep well if others only think about working and making money. Not everyone is true to their word.

THE GRILL. 123

You should have a small grill under the bar or counter, or in the best place, for serving fast foods such as toast, meat for sandwiches, etc. Watch out: the grill must be cleaned after every use so the different flavours don't mix. This grill will produce smoke and so it's best to put a small extractor fan above it. When you use the grill, you have to put on the extractor so the smoke doesn't bother the customers. This will be used frequently when there is no-one in the kitchen which makes us responsible for the customer. As I always say, customers are the ray of sunshine who must come in every day of the year. They are what allow us to grow and prosper and so we have to take care of them.

MICROWAVE OVEN. 124

You can have a microwave in the café to heat up any kind of food or drink quickly. A portion of food taken from the shelves in the counter can be heated quickly while you're making the customer's drink. When there are many customers, the kitchen can be the staff's third arm. In summary, both the grill and microwave at the counter perform a great service though at certain times, the kitchen is essential.

ICED DRINKS MACHINES IN VIEW OF THE PUBLIC. 125

The sale of these products in common in cafés, and the machines has to be visible at the counter. They'll be used throughout the day, making iced lemonade or whatever other drink they contain. They can also have coffee, orange juice, lemon juice, *horchata* or any other exotic drink. They have small blades inside which go round, scraping the frozen walls which produced the shaved ice. At the same time, they serve drinks and call the attention of the customer. When closing at night, the drinks left inside can be collected in a cup and put in the fridge. The machine is cleaned and prepared for the next day to be sure it will work again. First thing in the morning, the drink is put back into the machine, you start it up and the drinks are ready to be served, already cold and liquid. Iced coffee in some places isn't popular because they don't do what they need to to make money. The raw material isn't expensive. The machine is working and if the price isn't attractive to customers, it keeps on working without selling a much and making profits. Remember that low prices bring high numbers of sales. You should fill the till every day, remembering that many small sales is better than few large sales spaced out. The first will increase your sales while the second will decrease them.

AMOUNT OF COFFEE NEEDED FOR ICED COFFEE.126

It's a matter of intelligence. A coffee made in an Express coffee machine with twice as much water and lots of sugar will sell well. If you put a sign up announcing a good price for the customers to see, you'll sell a lot of iced coffee. The cup you use to serve it must look quite big and hold an average amount. Iced coffee is coffee with added water and sugar. You can have other plastic cups for taking out, planned in advance. Planning is vital: no battle is won without planning. The coffee can be prepared the night before. The water added can be cold or room temperature. Once prepared, put it inside the fridge and the next morning, put it in the ice machine which can turn it into iced coffee. Throughout the day, according to how much iced coffee we need, we can add more from our supply in the fridge. They are very slow in production so you have to pay attention in advance.

VARIOUS FLAVOURS OF SYRUP FOR USE IN ICED DRINKS. 127

Food and drink suppliers sell concentrated syrup with lemon, orange, *horchata*, blackcurrant, strawberry and many other flavours. You can also look through the Yellow Pages and find syrup factories or wholesalers from which you can buy them at low prices. In Spain, in Valencia,There are places where you can buy syrups. With three-quarters of a litre of syrup and 500 grams of sugar, you can make 8 to 10 litres of a drink ready to be iced. However, you can make better quality drinks by putting more syrup and less sugar to sell more and make any drink more competitive. You have to find the happy medium at a good price, cold and sweet. You can't get that coldness through the machines that the public usually see. It has to be done as I explain it. The liquid already cold when put in and then with the flakes of ice added in the machine. When customers tell you it's very sweet, tell them we'll work on improving it, and carry on as you were. There are some who do it with two-litre bottles of orangeade or lemonade which they sell to the public to try. To do this yourself, choose a mid-range bottle of orangeade, add sugar, taste it until it's really sweet, then add it to the machine. You'll be surprised at the cost. You should always have the liquid ready and in the fridge so that the machine can be topped up whenever needed without losing it's coldness.

THINKING LIKE A FACTORY IS VERY GOOD FOR BUSINESS. 128

A catering business starts earning money when it starts thinking like a factory. If you want to make a popular product, choose one which is currently selling, make it into a better price and advertise it in your business with an attractive sign that says: "A glass of this, this much money". If you sell at good prices in public opinion, you'll sell more while your general expenses will be almost the same. You'll also hav a higher profit because when you sell more, the normal profits you were getting earlier cover the general costs.

ICE-CREAMS. 129

All catering businesses sell ice-creams. Selling them in units is more practical. Soft serve ice-cream sold in bulk, served in cones, is also useful to sell. You can serve very attractive desserts using this. Buy a few photos of various ice-cream desserts from catering suppliers, work out the cost of each product yourself and set the sale price with a wide enough profit margin. Forget about the competition. Ignore their prices - work on your own ideas. If you copy something, improve on it. With your ice-cream photos, do what you do with your other dishes, add a few adornments to make them look better, and cover them with chocolate or whatever else you find in bakery suppliers.

COMPETING USING ICE-CREAMS. 130

The freedom to set your prices at what you want is the best invention for making money. Quality and good service are complementary to any sale. If you're in a street with a lot of people and the fridge with the ice-creams in is on view to all who pass, you'll sell a lot more than if you have it inside the shop. This needs to have a member of staff there with it. If you have to leave the counter to go outside to sell something, you might not get so many sales. You can get a lot of sales if you invent a really impressive "ice-cream of the day" to sell at the fridge and also at the counter, either in cones or plastic containers to take away.

THE TILL. 131

This must be away from the public at the hands of your staff. A good place is the wall at your staff's back when they are facing the customers. The night before, make sure that you have change in coins and notes for the next day so you don't have to go out to get more during work hours. It should print out receipts along with the date which are given to customers when they pay.

SPIRITS. 132

Bottles of spirits are usually located in solid and decorative shelves at the back of the assistant (on the wall) in view of the public near to the café. This wall can be made of ceramic so it is easy to clean. Here you can have both used and unopened bottles used for serving customers. The shelf and the bottles need to be cleaned every day since the customer will see them when he is at the counter. You can say that this partially represents the first impression of your business. If it is organised and clean, the customer will say: "It's very clean here!" and your business will work well. Cleaning is very easy. Take the bottles off the shelf, put them on the counter, clean the walls one by one with a dry cloth to remove the fingerprints and dust that can gather there, and then you put the bottles back.

The more common spirits, which are served more often, are those with which you can compete, with which you can serve with dispensers to get more profits. You will have seen these before. They are very simple, hung on the wall upside down and dispensing a set amount of alcohol each time. Just put the glass underneath and push the lever and the glass will be filled automatically. If you like the idea, you can use it with others. For good brand spirits, they are usually filled directly with your bartender's eyes as the only guide. It's very easy to lose money like this. You can resolve this by having large glasses which have two or more decorative horizontal lines so that you know where to fill up to. If the customer asks for more, you fill up to the second line and charge what they drink.

SPARE GLASSES AND BOTTLES. 133

Underneath the bottles of spirits you use to serve, you can keep the glasses to be used with them, and underneath those, you can keep spare bottles which you can have to avoid having to go to the store to get more if you run out. You must always make sure that the shelves have attractive bottles or packets of whatever. It's better to have your shelves empty than full of horrible-looking things. When you close up each night, you should restock this little store you have below the shelf. Also make sure there is a price list for all spirits, wines and other products to avoid confusion there in the shelves and another under the bar or counter for those moments of doubt.

GAMIN GENTERTAINMENT MACHINES. 134

Slot machines and other games machines are provided by authorised companies to for use in pubs or cafés. These companies are responsible for repairs and they collect the money inside. The owner of the pub pays nothing more, providing only the premises themselves and the electricity, and sharing the profits 50-50 with the company.
Repairs, taxes and anything else related to the working of the machines is the responsibility of the company which owns them. They usually come back once a week, take out the money, use a machine to count it in front of the owner and share it there and then. If there is enough space in the premises, put a pool table and table football game. The profits from these are also usually split 50-50. You could also choose to buy these since they are not electronic.
These kinds of games, electronic or not, are subject to very few taxes. Taxes on slot machines are very high and it has to be clearly expressed in the contract signed with the company that they pay them. If it is not put clearly in the contract that the machine owner is responsible, the tax office will charge

the owner of the pub with the machine inside if there is some kind of investigation. These companies will loan money against the profits made from the machines if necessary.

Some "distracted" customers will take advantage of the amount of customers and ask for a few coins to play with these machines agreeing to pay it back when they pay for their next drinks. Sometimes the staff member will forget to charge the customer for this extra, and this may end up being a substantial loss for the company. If a customer asks for coins, ask them for a note so you can change it for them. Tell the customer clearly that making change is something separate from drinks and so needs to be done separately.

SELLING TOBACCO. 135

In general, cigarette machines are installed by the owner of the cafés. Some catering businesses have contracts with companies that own them which should always be nearby. They are in charge of coming by every day to restock the machine and to withdraw the money taken. The owner and the supplier (either a tobacconist's or the company that supplies the tobacco) reach an agreement over the share kept by each party. For the owner of the café, this can be something useful.

Without needing to worry about anything, every month or whatever is agreed, you receive an amount of money free of charges, save that of the electricity. Some pubs sell cigarettes without a machine for prices as high as those of machines. Cigarettes sold in this way should be charged using a till straight away, so that you tell them immediately: "X amount of money", so you make it clear they need to pay you straight away without delay. If they didn't, many people would end up smoking for free. You have to avoid them telling you: "I'll pay you later", since they'll forget later. Very few people will say: "Hey, I haven't paid for these cigarettes".

If you are ever forced to go against this rule, write it down clearly in full view so that when you charge them later, you don't forget about charging them for the cigarettes too. If you don't trust your memory, it's very easy to forget. If you do this from the first day and don't let anyone owe you anything, you won't lose money or customers, and you won't have any problems. It's tough for anyone who doesn't like this system. They didn't have very good intentions.

GENERAL STORAGE. 136

The storeroom should be locked at all times. If it is left open, there is no stock control. The key can be kept in the till or in the supervisor's pocket, who will know when and who to let have it. You can keep bottles, food and other stock here that you want to be controlled, and not just left in anyone's hands. It's necessary to control what comes out of the storeroom to know how much you have in there. Stock control can be essential for making sure that you don't run out of anything.
When you run out of stock because it isn't controlled and there is no-one in charge of it, nobody will be to blame. If there is space, you can have a chest freezer for storing frozen products. When stock is delivered, it can be put in the door of the storeroom and wherever is convenient. It should be received by at least one employee. Only those related to your business should be allowed to enter the storeroom.

CONTROL OFFICE. 137

A small room should be enough for administration of the business which should also be kept locked. It could have one or two tables and a chair, filing cabinet, computer, a couple of lockers and whatever else you think necessary. It all depends on the size of the room and the business. You can put a small safe, mounted in the wall or the floor which can be hidden so that only the owners of the business know where it is. The fewer people that know, the better. In any business, certain unforeseen things can happen, which always occur because someone had access to the office.

Don't take cash from the safe in front of anyone to pay any bills or wages. It's better to pay with cheques. If you have to take something from the safe and someone else is there, invite them to go and drink something at the bar and you'll be with them in a minute. Always make sure no-one sees you when you open the safe and make it your secret, even if there is nothing valuable inside. Never have meetings or make payments or anything like that in your office.

You'll always have some table or a corner of the business where you can do what you need to. Your office is only for you. This advice is very useful. As well as planning your administration there, you can complete whatever calculations you need to, invent new products and think. And I mean "think", because that is the most profitable thing you can do for your business. will work through the night. Or you can buy it frozen and half-baked, and you finish it by baking in your oven when you need it. I don't think that frozen food is a good idea. (Better quality, better customers)

The food you need prepared for breakfasts are done in the kitchen, like omelettes, mini-sandwiches, French toast, etc. They usually sell well first thing in the morning. These are the first things you prepare in the kitchen. If the cook isn't available at that time, learn how to do it yourself, get up as early as you need to and before you open the business, it'll be already settled. You'll open ready for war with the ammo you need. If you want to be one of the worst cafés, turn up at opening time without anything prepared and you'll be dead in the water until you have everything ready to serve breakfast.

You'll soon have time so as not to be a slave as some say. Your economic situation will grow quickly and it'll help you to value your time and money. You'll also learn to value yourself.

Serving a croissant from the day before is easy if you open it up, spread on some butter or margarine and put it on the grill. But the worst thing is if a customer says: "Hey! This isn't fresh!" Be careful. You're about to lose this customer. If there has been a mistake, apologise, take it away and serve him another fresh one if you don't want to lose him. You should also never make a sandwich with bread from the day before. If you don't do what we recommend, your castle will come tumbling down... What we want to do is trap the customer with his weaknesses and get into his head and pocket. You can conquer a city with good service, quality, price and charm. If we cheat our customers, they won't come back. If we get them addicted to our services, we'll have a business with many regular customers which will grow every day.

TOAST. 138

Toast made with pan or tin bread is very expensive, and you'll never be really competitive with those. You can and should have them in order to serve to people who prefer them, along with individual pots of butter and jam, at their normal price for customers that prefer them. In order to be competitive with toast, you need others with common bread at lower costs. Bread ovens can make this common bread and cut it automatically for bread with tomato and ham, which is popular in Catalonia. This can be useful, both for the ham and toast which is uniformly cut. You have to have them ready to be made on the spot when ordered. I'll leave normal toast there so you can think about it. If you study it well, there is money to be made.

HOW TO SELL A LOT OF "HOUSE TOAST". 139

You can make these with slices of normal bread, not too thin. Recipe: A loaf of bread, cut in diagonal slices around 1.5 cm long, more or less thick. Before putting them on the grill, butter the side that you are going to toast first with melted margarine using a brush. Then, paint the other side and turn it over. You should have the margarine on a plate or in a container near or over the grill so that it is almost melting or at least soft. You can also put on olive oil in the same way.

When the toast is ready, spread on some jam which you can buy in bulk in those large industrial jars which bakeries use. You can have two or three flavours that the customers can choose. This gives the customer better service and makes them feel more important. It's a psychological trick to distract them and convince them not to change anything.

If a business does its calculations correctly to sell a product competitively, a clever customer may come along who wants something changed. In this case, if they want something more of whatever is being good enough. According to the place, you may put filters and water purifiers between the supply and the coffee machine. If we need to put water into the coffee machine and there isn't any, if we put the vaporiser in a water container and open the inlet so the vapour can escape, when there isn't any vapour left, it will absorb the water in the container.

ORIGINAL CAFÉ. 140

A café sold lots of coffee quickly and at a good price...It wasn't very large but had a very long counter to serve customers. When the demand for the price-quality ration was excessive, in the interior of the building, there was a giant insulated tank connected to the water supply and the coffee machine. The tank had electric circuits inside which caused the water to always be on the verge of boiling. When the coffee machine needed water was provided by the tank and it never lost the necessary pressure. You might say, you could do that with an electric water boiler. You could, but only an industrial one of at least a hundred litres. This seems simple, like a piece of cake. Everyone knows how to do it once they've seen it. As you can see, I explain how to make businesses that sell a lot and make money. You could even put a butane heater underneath the tank. And when there are a lot of customers or the power goes off, we need to continue providing a service which others maybe can't. These are all ideas based on being the best and "lucky". Luck is the consequence of the accumulation of intuition and experience which you have to have in advance if you want to get far.

HOW TO SELL A LOT OF COFFEE. 141

You can sell coffee any time of the day and, with the lowest prices of any other business in the sector, your sales will keep going up. In a commercial area, making good coffee, black, white or whatever, you can become rich in a few years. Hold on! When we talk about low prices, we're not talking about selling to people sitting at tables. Table service with waiters has to be charged at a higher price on top of the price for buying at the counter. You'll also find in another section of this book how to sell a lot of chocolate. You already know what customers want: quality, price and service.

Lowering your prices is not always the deciding factor. Sometimes you can be more competitive

through other services, such as the toilets. Of course you want to sell a lot of coffee or breakfasts. We could possibly complement those with mini sandwiches with special bread at a well-studied price. Pastries left over at the end of the day can be frozen. Don't sell them to customers again. It's a shame not to take advantage of them! So let the staff eat as many as they want because, otherwise, they'll eat today's! Pastries from the day before can be eaten once frozen, or opened and toasted with margarine. The boss always has to give a good example by eating them too. With the bread from the day before, you can make French toast. The most expensive thing with this is the oil to fry them, so if you want you can use them to make breadcrumbs. You have to live by the saying "We never throw anything away here". Lead by example, because everyone will do what they see you do... Do you know what my uncle said who made a lot of money? "Nobody ever got rich by giving away or throwing away!" And I don't think you're ready to lose your time and money by throwing things away, right?

BREAD AND PASTRIES. 142

At the end of the evening, phone and order the bread and pastries that you need for the next day asking them to bring it first thing in the morning so that you have it available when you open. If not, look for another supplier or pick it up from their business. They Any successful business working with their boss's intelligence and employees' physical labour. Success and luck are the product of imagination and thought.

CLOSING TIME. 143

When it comes to closing for the day, while the business is still open, be alert that it stays as clean and tidy as possible. When the amount of work decreases and closing time gets nearer, one employee can be restocking the bottles and cleaning whatever they can. After you close the front door to the public, lock it and don't let anyone else in. (Some undesirables and robbers may try to enter at that time.) Take away all of the tapas and take them to the fridge in the kitchen. The cook will know what to do with them the next day. After breakfast, the cook can check them and make sure they're fresh enough and throwing away whatever isn't, put them on new plates and you have the new tapas for the day. There could be fried tapas which are made in the kitchen whenever someone orders them.

END OF THE DAY, CLEANING AND RESTOCKING. 144

Upon closing the business, restock the bottles and fridges, put empty glasses in their boxes, put new drinks at the bottom, so that the older ones are used first and don't go out of date. Clean the coffee machine, dishwasher and grill really well. All the dishes must be clean and in their place. If we have any milk or chocolate flasks, whatever is left over can be stored in the fridge and used first thing the next morning. All machinery and equipment used during the day must be cleaned. Counters, bars, windows, etc. and the premises in general must be cleaned completely for the following day.
During work hours, keep an eye on the levels of water in the flasks and coffee machine. As you will find out, the containers inside the coffee machine, etc. can be removed to be washed. Before washing, make sure you unplug them from the mains. Inside these containers are the electric resistors which keep the water warm. Only plug it back in when it has water inside. These water deposits evaporate due to the heat produced by the resistors. Remove all the water, clean the inside well and then fill it with clean water. This has to be done every day after the day finishes. If the resistors burn out because there was no water inside, you'll have to call a technician to repair it, you'll waste time without being able to use it and you'll have an extra bill. Forgetting to check water levels will bring you problems and lose you money.

THE TILL.   145

When the business is closed for the day, the first thing the boss or supervisor must do is cash up the till. Take the money out once it is counted, write down the sales, discount any change given, etc. The total will equal the total sales according to the till receipts. Remove the part of the paper with the daily sales, take it to the office to see which hours were busiest and so on. Then with time you can stop looking at it but only you will know this. The others will believe that you watch them using the receipts, which you could do since the shift times should coincide with the receipt information. At night, before leaving the business, make sure the till has plenty of change of all coins and notes so that you can open without problems the next day. If you leave the same amount of change every day, when you cash up each night, there's no doubt as to how much money there should be, besides the money taken through sales. Throughout the day, the supervisor or boss should always have enough change help out the staff when necessary. This means you won't have to go begging to other businesses nearby. The boss or supervisor should collect money from the till every so often, writing a receipt for how much has been taken to help with cashing up. This money will be written in the staff book of whoever takes it so that we know at the end of the day where all the money is. Memory doesn't work well in these cases - you can get confused. If you sell tobacco yourself, you can also take money from the till and restock the packets of cigarettes.

TAPAS AT THE END OF THE EVENING.   146

Some tapas don't keep very well after being made in the morning and so can't be served the following day. You can serve these cheaper towards the end of the day. When you feel it's the right moment, you can start giving a free tapa (of the ones you feel will go off before the next day) with every purchase. You can give this to them for free. In this way, we can avoid serving tapas which might not look so good the day after they are made, even though they would be OK to eat. As well as being good publicity, these free tapas will help increase your sales at the end of the day. Entrepreneurs have the obligation of making extra work and of not missing an opportunity at work.

IMPORTANCE OF WEARING UNIFORMS. 147

All employees have to wear uniforms and be neatly dressed. In general in catering, clothing is usually very similar in most places: a white shirt, black trousers or skirt, a light jacket in winter, black shoes, a tie or bow-tie or with the neckline open, depending on the weather. This is a suggestion although the business can create whatever uniform they like. But the classic look is usually the safest. Who pays for these clothes? In general, they are paid a monthly amount set apart from their salary for clothing, and the waiters are obliged to wear these white and black classic clothes. If the owner wants something more to their taste, he should be the one who pays for being something unusual.

THE IMPORTANT THING ABOUT CAFÉS. 148

The fundamental thing is to that everything that comes out of the kitchen must be freshly made, unless they are stews or tapas which are prepared in advance and kept in the display windows for later heating. When customers ask for something they can see in front of them, they hope it is good and nice. Therefore, they have to be served skilfully and elegantly. They are the people who will fill our till every day and, if they like the service, the product and the price, come back again and again, and recommend you to their friends. Customers who come back the next day or after some time may have forgotten the price, but they won't forget the service and quality.

MISTAKES IN THE ORDERS.   149

When the customer or waiter gets confused when taking the order and when serving it, the customer says: "OH! This isn't what I wanted", take the food away, tell them not to worry, bring the food they want and only charge them what they wanted. This will encourage them to come back. We'll probably end up using the other food anyway and we won't lose the customer. If we had charged the customer both meals, they would never come back again. If a customer breaks a glass accidentally, give them another drink and only charge them for one. The next time they come back, we'll get the money back from the profits they give us next time they come back.
 The customer will keep coming. You just need to swallow your pride and take the hit. This customer and all the rest will help your company's tradition grow. If they drop it to the ground as a joke and it breaks, don't lose your cool. Act as if you didn't see it. If you get angry, it will only hurt your business. Others will even take advantage and leave without paying. Anyway, what really matters to you, like any other entrepreneur, is to earn money, right? Well, this is when you need to use intelligence and cool. Who knows if they wanted to create an incident so that they could steal something while you're away from the counter? It wouldn't be the first time. I remember there was once an armed robbery at a bank. They set fire to a building near to the bank so the security guards were busy with that while they robbed the bank. "Give me a

bottle of such-and-such a drink", asked one customer. It's not very common that a customer asks for a bottle and serves themselves but it could be that it's a custom in the place you are. If that's the case, give them an unopened bottle so you can see what they've had. If they leave about half, charge them as if they were glasses they'd drunk at the bar. You could do the following; serve a litre of sangria or draught beer in a jug for two or three people. This is normal in many places: why not set this in your business if no such custom exists?

You have to know in advance if you want to do this and charge the normal price, not more, so that the customers come specifically to drink with you from other parts of the city. You could even see if it is worth serving a few tapas with the service. You could have special prices, studied in advance, for those who buy bottles to take away. These bottles give you less profits that selling glasses, but you'll get even less if they go somewhere else to buy it. If customers know that there are drinks to take out and they aren't too expensive, they'll buy them more than once.

OTHER ITEMS TO TAKE AWAY.   150

If your café has enough staff in the kitchen, you can offer meals or tapas to take away. Paella, for example, is a popular and profitable dish. It is prepared in plastic dishes or packages wrapped up. You can also have cups for cold drinks or coffee with a small plastic spoon, or plastic cups to hold a litre of beer or sangria with a lid to be taken out. It's hard to have the paella ready when ordered, but it can be done when ordered and served in dish or pan directly, charging the per pan, or served in a plastic package to be used and thrown out. You can make the paella while they are drinking a beer.

My entrepreneur friend, there are many products which if we study them well, we may find millions of ways to sell more.

This idea of creating more work shouldn't be done by anyone except you, since your employees will feel like they're doing enough and will get angry at having to do more. When we talk about take-away food, it's important to study it well so as not to cheat your customers. Of course, you also have to do the corresponding adverts with signs in view of the public.

CHAPTER 4   151

RESTAURANTS WITH TAKE-AWAY FOOD   152

Serving meals and sandwiches. The sales of cooked food has been updated in many parts of the world. More customers are getting used to taking food away every day due to lack of time. Every small business can become big with a bit of originality, and here we don't want to be just another business in the pile. We can be the best. This type of food are popular, so any cook or cooking assistant must know how to do them.

PREMISES AND LOCATION. 153

The premises are important, but the location is much more so. In this case, a good location means one which many people pass, whether it be the commercial area of a town or village, or a certain area of a city. The installations you have inside the business should always be in proportion and agreement with the business's focus. In this case, simple and functional is enough. A place located in a strategic location for sales will be more expensive to rent but much more profitable than those cheap ones where nobody goes by.

Cheap location: little money to pay, little money to earn. If you're experienced in businesses, you can plan other new businesses in more doubtful locations if you feel you're capable of making people come to you, even if it is not in their normal area. These risky locations are good for experienced businessmen and whenever their money situation allows it, but new entrepreneurs must always be cautious and set up in good locations.

LAYOUT OF THE PREMISES. 154

Catering businesses have the same basic layout. They have the layout of the business they want to run as the premises allows them to be. For a take-away restaurant, between seventy and a hundred square metres should be enough. Some have very small premises but in very good locations for sales. In these take-away businesses, you don't need toilets for the public, but you do for the staff as we saw in previous chapters. There should be a counter separating the public from the rest of the business. (At least, that's how it's been up to now.)

The essentials for this business are the kitchen, toilets, changing room for staff, storeroom and the public area. If you want to serve food to people sitting down, as well providing take-aways, you need bigger premises. The layout always depends on the premises itself. Approximate sizes: 10 m for the kitchen, 12 m for the public toilets, men and women. 12 m for staff toilets and changing rooms, 8 m for the storeroom, 6 m for the office, and the rest of the premises for the public areas for taking out and for eating in. We've got an approximate distribution size here since the final word will always belong to the technician with the agreement of the owner, always abiding by the local laws. You could always hire a pub and set it out to achieve our aims. In a later chapter, I have written the approximate layout of a premises of 200 m2. In summary though, there is no law which says how you have to set it out.

ESSENTIAL EQUIPMENT FOR TAKE-AWAY RESTAURANTS. 155

The product being sold should be displayed in windows, closed on the customer's side and opened on the staff side. A microwave can be used to serve this food when necessary. A till with scales included which shows the price of the goods being weighed when you type in the price per kilo. A slicing machine. Shelves for products such as bottles, bread and so on. A fridge with large or small bottles of cold drinks. In part of the counter used to separate the public from the rest of the business, there should be shelves underneath for tools, packages and lids, plastic bags and other useful equipment. The walls should be painted with light colours. Strong colours, gadgets and other extremes show vulgarity and don't fit in this type of business. As we said about pubs, the lower parts of walls should be ceramic.

PRODUCTS AND SELLING TO THE PUBLIC. 156

Customers, upon entering the business, will find enough space for several people at the same time, a counter fronted with glass display windows, showing trays of cooked food, ready to be served. There can be various types of salads, stews, chicken, fish... and the most popular foods sold in the region. Each tray should show the price per kilo or per gram. Trays of hot stews can sit behind these windows, either being kept warm or cold, ready to be reheated at the choice of the customers. You can also have fresh meat pies, fish, croquettes and other types of hot fresh food that the customer can have cooked on the spot which will be out of the kitchen in a few minutes. You can have different types of cheese, ham, and other cold meats with their prices, ready to be cut, weighed and served. These fridges can also contain small amounts of vacuum-wrapped cold meats. You should also have some house desserts on display, such as flans, rice pudding or yoghurt, wrapped in plastic, etc.

Some types of fresh bread and pan bread. These exact specification may be different in every situation and location. It all depends on the entrepreneur and what they feel will sell well.

There can be plates of cold meats or salads within the fridges, prepared and ready to cover, weigh and take away. Salads mustn't have dressing so that the customer can decide what, if anything, they want on it. These salads without dressing will keep well in the fridge... Everything you sell can be put in packages closed with lids and we can sell them at the price of the food. All companies do it like this, apart from those that wrap them in paper, all-in-one packages or price decided by unit. There are infinite foods which can be easily sold. A sign to be put up saying: Products to be fried or completed at the request of our customers.

KITCHEN FOR THESE SPECIALITIES. 157

This must be connected to the service counter. It is also the law that you must have a vent to allow the smoke to escape through the roof too. It must have good connections to the water mains and sewers. An industrial fridge-freezer which doesn't necessarily have to be in the kitchen - because of the proximity to the heat - with enough space for food and various shelves. A cooker with various hobs which should be mixed, gas and electric, to be safer and to be able to cook various meals at the same time. There must also be deep fat fryers, one for fish, and another for meat, potatoes and so on. You should fry chorizos and other foods with strong flavours in a small pan with almost no oil. This will ensure that customers don't say that all their food tastes the same which will happen otherwise. You also need a dishwasher big enough to take pots and pans. An industrial oven for grilled chicken, meat, fish, pizzas, pasta and many other things, and some tables to work comfortably. You also need to leave a space for a bin which can be easily used and won't get in the way. Casserole dishes, frying pans and other kitchen equipment, some quick-cook pans, shelves for other necessities, and enough dishes and cutlery if we serve food at tables. About ten or twelve metres should be enough for this kitchen.

FOCUS OF THE BUSINESS. 158

The type and quality of food decides the customers we are selling to. To sell lots of food with this type of business, we have to be aware that the customers who go to this type of business are usually working- or middle-class people, although it's always possible to find people with more money. The food should be good home-made food at an average price, while it's preparation and presentation should the best they can be.

It's not the same to throw food at customers as to serve it to them. The difference here is very important. When we are served food, we want to be served cleanly and skilfully as well as being well-prepared. The staff's clothes and cleanliness have to impeccable. People eat with their eyes more than with their wallet. The white aprons, jackets or shirts of the staff must be perfectly clean every day.

HOW CUSTOMERS ACT. 159

When the customer enters our business, he will have a look around the premises without fixing on anything in particular. He goes to the displays windows and looks at the food and prices. He'll now work out how much food he wants to buy and, sometimes, the amount of money he can or wants to spend. If we put a sign which says the price per kilo and underneath: "Individual portion, 200 grams, so many euros", the customer may think that by buying per portion, he can have a more varied meal. In every business, you have to think like a customer and what we'd be looking for. Above all else, we'd think about quality, variety and money! The customer chooses the food he wants to buy and the staff will start making the order. Depending on what he orders, he will put it on the scales, weigh it, cover it and write the cost down wherever convenient. You add the totals together in the till using the scales and find the total to charge. If they ask for some food which needs to be finished, such as fish or meat, send it quickly to the kitchen so that they do it right away. The kitchen will always have the cook ready to make the food, with hot oil or the grill ready.

Once the order has been weighed and valued, put it in a bag with handles and give it to the customer together with their receipt.

If we put up a sign which says: "Dear customers, you may taste whatever food you like", the ones that have doubts over whether to buy the food can try it and, whether or not they buy it, it helps with publicity... This will consist of a spoonful of the food they choose in a saucer, along with a spoon or fork. This expense is important for publicity and will help increase sales. From then on, some people will come back if only for that reason.

Careful! In some businesses, since the cook is so good, they will try every food before buying something.

Here, there is no room for apologies. The food must be prepared correctly. It's better that it has too little salt than too much. If a customer takes food away with no salt, they can eat it anyway or can put on their own. If it's too salty, it can't be fixed and they'll have wasted their money. They may bring it back to get a refund, or throw it away. Either way, they won't come back. That day will be the beginning of the end. All staff should be obliged to try the food before selling it, as an extra responsibility. Also be careful that the food isn't burnt or stuck to the bottom of the pan. In this case, it can't be fixed and must be thrown away. This should be taken as a lesson learnt.

Food has to be perfect in presentation, quality and taste.

Some customers will come with other people and you may need to put some seats for those who are waiting. Everything I recommend here is to be different and competitive. Being competitive doesn't just mean lowering the prices. Sometimes it is better to keep them the same. It always means giving a good general service. It's very common that some entrepreneurs, because they are good cooks, think that that's enough for their business to go well. The most important thing in any business is that the customers come back. The first time, they'll come in because they are curious. Every other time will be because they are happy with the price, service and quality. Customers want the best quality and price, and to be served well. Not just the first time but every time. Surprise your customers with new ideas and meals every now and then.

WHAT THE CUSTOMER SEES WHILE BEING SERVED. 160

When a customer is making an order, he watches the food as it is made, how it is handled and the general cleanliness. The staff must be true actors. The customers' "cameras" are recording everything they see. If the staff are not well dressed, the customer remembers that. If the shelves or something else are not tidy, presentable and clean, they will remember that too. The staff in the business have their put themselves in the customer's place and see if everything is clean and tidy, including the windows and trays of food.

THE STAFF'S ABILITIES. 161

In all businesses which use scales to measure food, the customers are used to the weight not always being exact. The customers knows that cooked food which costs a certain amount by its weight will be almost perfect and that you won't charge them any extra since the scales work out the correct price. In the greengrocer's, if you look for the perfect fruit to make exactly a kilo, it will take a lot of time. You end up charging by the actual weight of the fruit. In these cases, putting a little more or less doesn't matter to us. If the weights are not fair, the result at the end of the day is that we will have sold a little more.Staff must take into account that if the tray of food is wet with its juices, or if it is badly handled, it's better to put it into the back of the business, change the tray and make it look as new. The effect of the cleanliness can make the customer into a regular. When we have our prices in view of customers at all times, we are showing them that it is a trustworthy business. Hiding prices, according to most customers, is a way of cheating the customer. Even if you don't charge too much, they'll always have their doubts and avoid buying where they can't see the prices. Clear and visible prices can multiply your sales and nobody will doubt the business's honour.

MANAGING THIS BUSINESS. 162

The food you sell, from the first day, has to be perfectly prepared by people who know the trade. Preparing really tasty food doesn't necessarily require the most expensive products at the market since a professional cook knows how to get the best out of cheaper products. If you plan to run this as a family business and you're not an expert, I recommend that you hire an experienced cook who knows this job well. When we've learned enough, if we don't need this employee, we can do without them. You can also hire a professional to help start up the business and then get a good cookbook to start inventing new meals. However, any employee should be in the kitchen. All contact with the public should be sales staff and the owner himself.

TRADITIONAL MEALS FROM THAT AREA. 163

Some meals you serve can be popular traditional one and after two or three, you'll have learned enough. But if you need an employee, it must be for the kitchen. With kitchen work, it must be understood that when cooking is finished for the day, everything must be left tidy and impeccably clean. The kitchen is very important but the public-facing side of the business is no less so. The entrepreneur, or the person who attends the customer, must be a salesperson. They must always be ready to tolerate customers' bad moods. As I said before, thestaff are actors who fulfil a role and have to do so perfectly. Customers are the source of funding which keep the business going and a good salesperson who wants the best for the business is the best person to keep customers coming back. If they are women, you can help them with a little commission. Well, what I say here is half-true; some female staff are very good salespeople. Never forget that a good salesperson can sell anything. A bad one, on the other hand, can ruin any business.

PACKAGES FOR FOOD. 164

Packages to take away food are usually plastic and lightweight. There are various types in different sizes, since each manufacturer has their own versions. You can have various sizes to hold different things with their corresponding lid (in which you can put anything from a coffee to a roast chicken). Some can be deep for stews or liquids, and others shallower for salads and hors d'oeuvres. The package is sold at the price of the food, and you'll have no problem in getting the money back with your profits. You can also have bags to take away food and other packages which can be used depending on your needs. At first, you should get a few of each since we don't know which will be most useful to us.

SALES AND WORK HOURS. 165

In catering business, such as cafés or pubs, sales hours are very wide. Each one chooses the timetable most suitable for them. For example, you could be open from twelve in the morning until five in the afternoon. It all depends on the Part 2 country and customs of where you are. At night, sales drop quite a lot, and you may choose different timetables for the time of year. This is not a lot of time to sell, so you have to take advantage of them as much as possible. If, after closing, a customer calls for you to serve him, it could be an opportunity to sell whatever was left over. If you do, he may come back. In this case, you'd need a window so that he doesn't enter the building.

You must have the door locked to avoid burglars getting in and ruining the day. If there are no windows, put a strong chain which wouldn't break with a strong kick, and you can serve him through there. When closing time approaches, sales will go down.

You can use this time to start tidying and cleaning whatever you can. When you close up, a new battle starts: general cleaning. In catering, it is tradition that the business be clean overnight, and the food be stored in the fridge or freezer. In self-service businesses, I've already explained how to store the meals, and it can be frozen, as I mentioned, so that you can serve the same food the next day. What do we do with the left-over food? If they are stews, they are kept after being boiled and cooled. Other foods are kept in the fridge or wherever the boss thinks convenient.

STUDY, OFFICE AND SO ON. 166

You should find the tools and furniture necessary to have all admin documents, lists, price calculations, etc
STOREROOM.   In this room, you can have shelves for food, drinks and other products necessary for the building, as we explained in the café chapter.

OPENING DAY. 167

When a business of this type is opened, on the first day, the people who come through the door will look around to find out what is being sold. If they see the building well lit, plenty of space for customers and sparkling windows, they'll go to look at what they have behind them. They'll look a everything, check out the food, prices and presentation. They'll compare them to other similar places they've seen, working out if there are better prices and variety. Some may buy something, others won't.

THE VITAL MOMENT OF THE CUSTOMERS' VISIT. 168

At the moment in which the customer enters our business and it looks like he's seen everything, the staff have a few seconds to approach them and ask if they want to taste anything. Don't wait for them to answer. You say with a nice smile: "Which would you like to try?" It's a psychological way to get them involved which they can't reject.
A saucer and spoon with a couple of spoonfuls of that food and a little wine or another drink in a small glass, with a tray to put their cutlery on. If all your food is gone on that first day, mostly through invitations, that will have been a great day. And it's worth putting a sign outside saying: "Today,

taste our home-made meals (free)". Many people will enter even if just for curiosity's sake. They are like flies - when they land on the honey, they are stuck.

The kitchen has to be well-prepared to finish any other orders. Some unforeseen things will happen which, if they are not resolved at that moment, will make us look bad to the customers. The food you want to sell must be kept cold. There should be a certain amount of food for the tasting, either hot or cold. Other customers might choose some cold salad which you can serve as you sell it. Salad is a very popular menu and you can have a huge variety in small quantities when it is good for you. You can have only half the full amount of presentation trays which will make your customers believe that they've been selling.

PUBLICITY AND SELLERS. 169

Advertising forms part of the business plan. Some customers will buy something and others won't, but that doesn't matter. You'll still have a positive advertising campaign. At first, you need to have the help of someone who knows how to sell well until you can see how the business is going. The important thing is to serve all the customers who come in to taste or buy, and not look stupid. Be careful that all staff who are customer-facing have to be wearing a nice, clean uniform. The first impression that you give the customers is of hugely importance so that the business starts off on the right foot. If you invite people to eat for free, make sure you get rid of all your food.

Give business cards to every customer thanking them for their visit. The next day, some might come in who didn't come for the tasting. They can try for free anyway. Many who did come in on the first day will come back to buy something. Every day of the year, if any potential customer is unsure about which food to try, you can suggest they taste it.

Hot foods (in general) are kept cold on the appropriate trays. You can ask each customer if they want to take any hot food. Put them in the microwave and they're done. The first things you prepare will be those that need to be heated, and while they're in the microwave, you can complete the rest of the order.

TRADE NAME. 170

The name of the business should be short and easy to remember for customers. It may be a short number which quickly becomes popular. You can invent a name which is made of only one word or two written together, easy to remember. After a little good publicity, soon your customers will have your name on their lips

EAT-IN RESTAURANTS.   171

Let's imagine you want to serve food to tables in the same restaurant where you have take-away food. The taxes will be the same for the restaurant. If we have enough space to have table service, we would also need, by law, public toilets. We can serve food on ceramic plates, or something similar, and stainless steel cutlery; using plastic here for this service would be harmful to the business.

Every business has opportunities to sell, and it's a question of being able to take advantage of them. The food served can be the same as the take-away food and maybe some others if convenient. Exactly the same food but served to tables. This service can be economic up to a certain point. We still need to serve with care to show our class. Offers can take the form of a menu choosing between two or three starters, main courses, a normal dessert, (a glass of water or wine, or any other drink we can get at a good price), a portion of bread and a price which we've worked out well in advance, so we don't waste time standing around. You could also have a menu with other dishes as well as the menu of the day, such as hors d'oeuvres, special salads, desserts, beers, drinks and others with their prices.

In a normal restaurant, when serving the menu of the day, they include a ¼ of a litre of wine or water. So, why shouldn't we be any different? Of course, if we put a beer with a good price on the menu, and we want to earn money as in other businesses, it won't go as we expected. For example, if another restaurant serves, as we said, wine or water in the menu and, without changing the price, we serve beer or more wine, we'll be competitive. Like in all businesses, before making an offer, it's important to study the price well so that if our competitors change their prices, we are able to resist and continue. One idea that comes to mind to beat our competition and increase sales is: Chicken or beef bones or other remains, together with a few vegetables could be the ingredients for a good broth when given appropriate condiments. We can gain more customers by offering free bowls of the house broth to people who have already made their order (and not before). If we make enough stew, we can sell it to take away at a moderate price (it's very cheap to make). Prepare an appropriate package so it doesn't spill, because you'll sell a lot. The best way to keep this broth and have it ready to serve is to keep it in a flask (as we explained in the café section). Some customers may ask for another bowl. You have to expect this and let the customer know, nicely, that the second bowl will be charged. If we put in the menu "Bowl of house broth, X cents", we'll be OK. Don't forget that you'll make a lot of money if you can interpret the ideas you read.

ONE SWALLOW DOESN'T MAKE A SUMMER, BUT IT'LL HELP YOU OUT. 172

You have to plan everything in advance cleverly. If a customer who comes in to buy a meal and we have a self-service restaurant, he already knows how it works as we'll see in a later chapter. The impact a customer gets when taking away food is completely different. It has to be. If the food you sell is moist and appetising, the customer will see good service. To be sure of a good service, we can invent a completely different system even with the same food. If we have the food repeated inside the kitchen, we can take the order from the customer who comes to the counter, take it to the kitchen and he will get it hot. These are things to consider. Another idea is to have a long the take-away food counter which will also serve food to tables, as described in the self-service chapter. This would be an extra service and give more opportunity to sell things. It's something for the entrepreneur to think about. Don't forget that you have to think like a customer before a businessman, because this will help you increase sales. With good customer service, the amount of money taken per day can be doubled.

ROTISSERIE FOR CHICKENS ON VIEW. 173

Some people have chicken rotisseries on the wall in view of the public which is also good publicity for the business. These rotisseries are usually gas or electric. It's easy to manage them. You can also have some roasted chickens ready to sell. Chickens cut in halves or quarters can be sold. You can also have more chickens in the kitchen ready to serve. Every entrepreneur can choose the working method they like. The company AVIDESA in Valencia (who we used to buy from) or any other company supply frozen chickens over the whole of Spain, in boxes with either eight or ten units. They are clean, ready to roast and eat. There are units which weigh half a kilo, three quarters or a kilo, and maybe other sizes too. They are good to work with and fit in with your company well. You can find similar services in any other place. There may also be other cheaper services which require more work. Roast chickens left over at the end of the day can be frozen and sold another day. You can also try chicken salads, chicken pasties, and various other products which the cooks will know how to make. We don't throw anything away here.

SPECIAL TRAYS FOR FREEZING. 174

Plastic trays from six to eight centimetres high, of a manageable size, which can be stacked, can be very useful for keeping food in the fridge. Keep each one with its lid and you can put them in the fridge and take them out easily. When the working day is finished and some food is left over which is fine to eat, you can boil it, cool it down with cold water and once it is cold, put it in one of those trays we were talking about. Label it with the day and contents, and put it in the freezer. They keep well for a few days until that food is served again. Then you can take it out, boil it quickly and prepare it for sale. It should be the first one you sell that day without mixing it with other food from the same day. We have to be sure they are good. Other foods can also be frozen. The cook will know what is the best thing at each moment. Having good fridges and freezers is essential since they are vital to the economic state of your business. Pieces of fish, birds or meats which don't look very good but are perfectly edible can be frozen as we explained and can be kept for other foods, such as croquettes or the fillings for pies and pasties. As a last resort, maybe for the house broth. This is something which will help your business be a success. You can read about the matter of premises, the best way to get a good rental contract, and the choice of location in the first part of this book.

CHAPTER 5   - 175

SELF-SERVICE RESTAURANT OR CAFÉ   176

This type of business is very easy to understand. The customers themselves choose the foot they want from everything offered at the restaurant. They place their order on a tray, take it to the till where they pay. Then they go to a table, sit down, eat and, once they've finished, leave. This is enough explicit explanation. As we said in the title of the chapter, either cafés or restaurants can use this system which can be available at all times.

These are opened in places with lots of people, such as roads or motorways, summer holiday destinations, commercial areas in large cities or smaller towns with lots of people, where people are very busy and have little time available. This type of business can sell more food in less time if the work is done quickly and efficiently enough. In other businesses, the serving times are very open. In this case specifically, the hours may be long but they are limited to the usual meal times, unless you specifically want a continuous service.

At dinner times, sales are slow and it isn't the best time to get a lot of money, apart from in big cities where you can get good sales at those times, as well as in the main courses. In these key hours, you have to work with the appropriate dynamic. The level of work for staff during meal times to key for gaining an acceptable amount of money and attending to all the customers. The amount of people at night, if it is a popular restaurant, will be quite a bit less than at midday, though it all depends on the location and type of business. In popular restaurants in large cities, dinner time starts at the beginning of the evening which is the right time for people who don't want to eat at home but have to go to work the next day. Others who don't have to get up early may go along too. These restaurants have to be located in the right location - commercial areas with lots of people. It doesn't necessarily need to be on the high street, but very close to it. In summer holiday locations, the opening and closing times can be decided by the owner depending on the time of year. The business needs to accept the customs of the place they are located. Sometimes, particular changes can be accepted by the public. It all depends on the entrepreneur's vision. We can put any work times we want depending on what is best for the business.

SELF-SERVICE, A SIMPLE SPECIALITY. 177

These restaurants are quite a lot simpler than normal restaurants. The personalised meals of à la carte restaurants don't exist here. The dishes offered each day can be different, depending on the owner and the cook. Many people go into these places. Some are regulars, others only every now and then, either for the prices or for how practical it is.
Price, quality, service and speed are important for good sales. There are also people who like to see the food before eating and like this type of service, as long as it meets their price and quality expectations. Future entrepreneurs must know that, in the right place, they sell a lot. I mention this because if you set up in the wrong place, you've already lost. By taking away the waiters bringing food to the tables, we also reduce the number of staff. Of course, we still need enough staff to cover every need. If it's in the right location, customers will be coming in continuously

ADVERTISING. 178

Many customers go to this kind of place. Advertising on walls in public areas or any other means in a city area will be effective. It's good that the general population know that your business exists, so much so that if travellers from other parts of the city or from outside the city ask for a self-service restaurant, anyone can tell them where you are. First recommendation: make sure all people in the area know you exist. Second: maintain a good level of service from the first day.

TYPE OF FOOD SERVED. 180

The variety of food offered each day can be two or three starters and so many other main courses. This is relative and relevant to how busy the business is, it may be much more or less. In this type of business, if there are no other laws, the customers may freely choose what they want and the till will charge them whatever they have in their tray. The businessman has to find ways of making mid-cost foods very well that look great...

GENERAL SUPERVISOR. 181

There must be one supervisor who controls everything that happens in the business, trying all food which is made and not tolerating any food which comes out of the kitchen which is not in a perfect condition. The head chef knows what has to happen when a mishap like this occurs.
The owner must have no doubts that when food is not good, it must be thrown away. Some restaurant owners breed pigs in some other location and feed them the leftover or wasted food since they can use the pork in the business later. If you have no experience in catering as a businessman, you'll learn quickly if you do everything enthusiastically. You can also be sure that you're doing the right thing and you'll be lucky. When you finish reading this book, you'll be prepared to run

any business I've explained with plenty knowledge.

WORKING-CLASS CONSUMERS. 182

It's good to make clear that most self-service restaurants are of mid-range quality for working- or middle-class people, since there are more people here and it's easier to be successful. You can also set up self-service restaurants with better quality where the price will be related to the service and the facilities. This is usually the case in five-star hotels. We can make a mistake if the business is not in the correct location for the type of business. If you want large amounts of sales, you have to make food the majority will enjoy. The location doesn't necessarily need to be in the most expensive and central places in the city, but they have to be near to large amounts people on foot or near places with lots of people. The most important thing, in this case, is to make food which is easy to make and not expensive. An experienced cook will know how to prepare them. You've already read what to do if you have never worked in this trade before. In terms of staff, you need a good organiser and a good cook.

The other jobs can be easily covered. Your job as the owner will be to be everywhere, never staying in one place, because in this way you'll make sure that the business is working and that everyone is doing what they should be. If you know what every one of your employees is doing, you'll be the master of it very soon. The boss should go in and out of the building as many times as he wants, helping with everything to make sure the business is working well. Don't let any one person do what they want without your supervision.

CUSTOMER ENTERS THE RESTAURANT. 183

When customers enter the business for the first time, almost all of them know what they will find. They'll see shelves with trays, and they'll take one so they can put what they want on it. They'll take the cutlery, which should be wrapped in napkins or cellophane bags. They pick up the bread they want (which we'll charge for too), either white or brown. There should also be paper napkins here or on the table, something else to bear in mind if the trays are the size of the tables.

DISPLAY COUNTER. 184

This consists of a row of various pieces of furniture, food containers which face the customer so they can take whatever food and drink they want to have. For those that need to be kept warm, below the trays of food, there is a type of sink with water kept hot by electrical resistors inside. For cold food, fridges can be adapted to this need. This is a brief explanation.
If you want to know more about this, ask about companies that install these pieces of equipment. Where? In the Yellow Pages, look for catering and industrial kitchen installations, or for the equipment distributors for caterers in your own town. You could always look for "Commercial Installations". They can install everything you need. It's good to see restaurants of this type working in large cities. This will help you a lot to decide what you want in your business.

SHELF TO PLACE TRAYS ON. 185

All along the display counter, at hand height, there should be a shelf which could be some kind of grate, metal or wooden bars, on which the customer can put their tray and push it along, putting on the food they want. When they are hungry, it all looks good and, if it's well-presented, they will fill their tray. Before eating, it all looks good. Then after they've paid and taken the food to the table, it's sold and we won't accept any refunds if they are full.

FOOD COLLECTION PASSAGE. 186

Between the food service bar and the rest of the dining room, at a distance of approximately one metre twenty centimetres, there will be a type of barrier which stops the customer from entering the dining room with their food without having paid for what they have on their tray. This forms a passage and could be made by a horizontal bar at a height of seventy or eighty centimetres from the ground. It can be made of stainless steel or wood, as if they were normal handrails. You could also put up some small posts with decorative chains, thick ropes, etc. There are many possibilities. The idea is that the posts shouldn't fall down and that they stay stuck to the ground, at low costs. These posts can be fixed to the ground with screws and bolts, and between each post, a chain or whatever it might be. In Spain, the company "TendíFlex, Proches S.L." makes posts and appropriate chains for these cases. Tel. 96 372 9862

COLD MEALS AND HORS D'OEUVRES. 187

You should have a fridge with various glass shelves and no higher than eye-level, open to the customer so that they can serve themselves comfortably, with or without a door on the staff's side. To allow the cold from below to work effectively, the shelves may be like a grill. You can have various salads, hors d'oeuvres, with asparagus, ham, cheese, olives, anchovies and so on. These individually-sized dishes are attractive and don't have too much food on. They can be used as hors d'oeuvres for some and starters for others. You need to compare the price and quantity with others to make sure it is at a fair price. Each plate should be no bigger than 20 cm in diameter and have the price visible. The customer will be looking and some will work out what they want to spend and what they can get with that money. Snacks can be put on saucers or dessert dishes. Whatever isn't visible won't be bought. Salads will keep better if they don't have any condiments on them. You also need to remember to have salt and pepper pots on the tables. It could also be on a small shelf which could be used for various tables. Something else for the owner to study.

FIRST COURSES. 188

Customer can choose the food they want as they go. You always need some variation in the menu because those that come in every day won't like seeing the same things all the time. Even so, the more common dishes can be used more often like, for example, paella with rice which can be used every day when convenient.

The first and second courses will be served in portions and by the staff. The customer indicates on the menu which they want and the staff give it to them, since this food has to be served correctly. Among the two or three starters you offer, you could include beans, vegetables, pastries, rice, stews and many others which are easy to make. Working-class customers prefer a good starter which fills them... You have to make sure that the food is being eaten before putting more. At the end of the day, there should be as few as possible left.

SECOND COURSES. 189

These include meats, such as beef, pork, chicken, fish, and so on, with appropriate garnishes. Food must be good quality at a good price, since that will decide the number of sales and the profits. You should decide in advance the amount of food in each portion, however if a customer wants a little more, without doubling the portion, you can allow it since they'll be the minority. Potatoes, pasta, rice, beans, vegetables and many other foods are common here. If you do paella, you need to do just the right amount so that not much is left over since it doesn't keep very well. Paella has to be very well prepared so that our gourmet customers will have no problems in coming back. It is a very common meal at a low cost. However, white rice can be boiled and kept in the fridge. Any cook knows this. Put the rice in water on the cooker, a pinch of salt, a laurel leaf and a splash of olive oil. Make sure it doesn't get soft. When it is al dente, drain the rice, run it under the cold tap until it is cold, then dry it and keep it in the fridge. This can stay in the fridge for two or three days. This isn't a cookbook - that's what you have the cook for - but it's always good for a businessman who's never worked in catering before to know a few dishes.

CHILDREN'S MENU. 190

You can have a special menu with half portions for children. Their prices should be lower than normal but never more less 75% of the main menu. Well, we don't need to decide that now. Our work will decide it for us. Children tend to eat food like macaroni, rice, croquettes, hamburgers, breaded meat and chips, though some do like vegetables. White rice kept in the fridge can sometimes keep children happy if they want paella and there isn't any. A good cook can improvise something nice for children with rice, imitating paella. Staff that give out food will decide when it is necessary to ask their father if they want to see the children's menu for that child. You can always prepare a small dish for children using the main menu. (Remember that if you treat the children well, they can make their parents come much more often.)

THE DESSERTS ARE NEXT. 191

These are kept in a fridge which can be opened by customers so they can get what they want. They can include pieces of fruit, slices of cake or pie, custard, yoghurts, rice pudding. Every one can be put on an individual plate. They should include a dessert spoon or fork, and can be placed in glasses. Ice-creams will be sold by unit, kept in the freezer, opened at the top by a transparent door, etc., so that the customer chooses what he wants. The prices must always be visible. If a client doesn't know how much something costs, he's afraid you'll rip him off when it comes to paying. On top of fridges opened from above, where the customer takes what they want, you can put some shelves with desserts which don't need to be so cold. You'd have to see the furniture you have to see what you can do with it.

AND THEN THE DRINKS. 192

Cold drinks should also be a fridge opened from above through which the customers can serve themselves. These include quarter- and half-litre bottles of sparkling or still water, half-litre fizzy drinks, and two or three types of beer in cans. Half-litre and three-quarter-litre bottles of white and red wines, and clarets, of the various brands depends on price and quality. You can also have various juices, milk-based drinks, cava and other drinks. You could also have a jug of sangria without ice as we've explained. You should also have a sign nearby showing the price of each thing. A jug of sangria as we've seen in early paragraphs. The jug should be half-full. Put it in the fridge with the cold bottles and a sign that says: "Ready-made sangria. Help yourself!

FILL IT WITH ICE CUBES UP TO THE TOP!" (AND THE PRICE). ICE CUBES. 193

In the same fridge, we have a container with ice cubes, glasses and tongs so that the customers can serve themselves. An ice cube making machine? You can have this in a place where there isn't much heat. Another option is to buy them ready-made and have a chest freezer to keep them in. Ice cube-making machines are worth good money, and often break down and have other small problems, which can be a pain. The best service thing is to buy the ice cubes if they're relatively easy to find. If not, buy the best machine you can find without problems and if the tap water in your area isn't suitable for drinking, the company should explain to you how to solve the problem. If this is the case, ask other people in the same trade what they did and what is the best thing to do.

Another option for you is to make the ice cubes yourself and sell them to other catering companies and the markets in general. This could be a good idea to seriously think about. In places where drinking water isn't very good quality, it may be interesting to consider that being in a hot, huge city, this type of business could be enormous.

STAFF IN CHARGE OF RESTOCKING. 194

My recommendation is that all employees should be watching that nothing is running low and that they know how to make sangria quickly, as well as order
the hors d'oeuvres and salads in the display windows from the kitchen. They should keep everything running so that sales don't stop. Restocking pots and trays of food in the counter, taking away empty ones, bringing the right number of clean plates so that the customers don't need to slow down. When used trays and dishes are taken from the tables, they go directly to the kitchen. If the distance from the centre of the

dining room to the kitchen is very long, open a window, if possible, directly to the kitchen or to the sink. Some businesses have a small conveyor belt on which trays can be put which leads to the kitchen. This can speed things up considerably when clearing tables. When the day is done, we keep the food left-over, doing what we talked about in the last chapter.

VISIBLE PRICES. 195

When a customer walks in, the first things they look for are the menus and prices. Knowing these helps them know what they want to spend or if they can afford it. They must easily find the price of every portion of food served that day, as well as the drinks, desserts, hors d'oeuvres and salads. Everything should be priced. They feel more comfortable and spend more money if they know in advance what they are spending. Any business owners who hide their prices are not very good. It's another way of conducting your business, but I don't like it nor recommend it. It's for dishonest businesses which don't display their prices and charge depending on what they think they can get. When we show the quality and price, it means that the price is related to what is being sold. Medium quality shouldn't be sold at high prices. Customers are experts at this.

COST EXAMPLES.. 196

As a starter, 100 grams (before cooking) of macaroni is enough for a good portion. If you add some fried onion or garlic, some ham or chorizo, at a good price, fried tomato and a bit of grated cheese, the price of this food will be the cheapest of all the ones you make.
Cooks are there to help us make a huge variety of pasta. Rice

and pasta are very profitable for the business and well-liked by customers. The important thing is to cook them well. There isno fixed price. Some will be cheaper than others. 100 grams of dry pulses should be enough for a portion. If we double the cost of them, this will give you the cost price including condiments. These are just simple comments which will help you understand where the profits come from. The best food for the price, besides pasta and rice, are chicken, pork, or other good-quality meats to be cooked, minced or breaded, pulses, some moderately-priced fish, vegetables, etc. A good cook knows how to make good, cheap dishes with these and other types of food. In only a little time, if the owner is not a cook when starting the business, he'll know how to invent dishes which are popular and profitable

CUSTOMER SERVICE. 197

Any person who enters the business to eat is responsible for your profits, and the ones who spend little are just as important as the ones who spend a lot. You must never be wrong with a customer, with the price nor the food. Customers are not idiots and before coming in, they will have been to many other similar businesses. Some businesses give away little food and get lots of money. How can that be? Serving very stingy portions and charging money which is not related to the quality and quantity.

Some businessmen in any trade want to make a fortune quickly and, when they don't get it, complain about their bad luck. This happens because they are so desperate to make money. Either they aren't intelligent and weren't well advised, or they haven't read anything about being successful and lucky. These entrepreneurs who think in this way don't often have good businesses. They are so eager for money, they forget about the basics like good hygiene and customer service, which are important for getting new customers.

SUCCESS DEPENDS ON INTELLIGENCE. 198

Honour and the spirit of sacrifice are essential to success. Trust people who are naturally good workers. They are generally honourable and are good travel companions in your business journey, but remember that your employees are employees and the boss is the boss. Remember that you alone don't have time to make money. Be clever and surround yourself with good staff. An employee with no interest in what they do will only hurt your business. You'll know what to do when this problem arises.

THE PREMISES WILL ALWAYS END UP BEING SMALL. 199

When we think about this kind of business, we have to have a large number of seats. We know the dining room could fill up with customers at meal times. Some will leave when they finish and others will take their places, but even so, if we don't have much space, we'll have few tables and it will be difficult to sell a lot.

FIXTURES. 200

In this kind of restaurant, we can make the dining room as nice as we want. The best thing is general is to make it simple, in good taste and spotless. I would never advise you to spend more money than necessary on fixtures. Luxuries are for places where they charge at luxurious prices.

MORE TABLES, OPPORTUNITY FOR MORE SALES. 201

Some things that work well for selling lots of food. When customers have finished eating, if you take their plates away, they will be very comfortable and might stay there chatting all afternoon, which will hurt the business. If customers ask for their plates to be taken away, tell them "I'll be there in a minute", but don't take away any plates, and they should leave soon.

Having more tables unoccupied is more profitable at meal times if other people come and sit at them. The exception is if you have so many tables that you can afford the luxury of people staying longer than necessary. This may seem like bad customer service but we can't tolerate giving good prices and quick service only to have them stay all afternoon chatting. That's what you have à la carte restaurants for which we talked about before. The price there includes the time for chatting or resting as well as the food.

IF CUSTOMERS ORDER COFFEE. 202

Those that want coffee at their table should go to the counter and go through the till as usual. In the area opposite the food counter (this is just an idea), you could have a mini counter with coffee, alcohol and other drinks which also ends in a till, using the same system as the food.

The staff that makes the coffee will also give the customer a neatly-presented note, specifying clearly the contents of the coffee and other drinks, since they are made at the request of the customer and may have variations. They take the coffee in a small tray and pay at the till as we have agreed in this company. You could also see if it is worth that same waiter charging for it. Tobacco will be inside a machine. People may also go back to the till for desserts. Some businesses may have a counter separate for clearing the tables when customers are finished eating. When they ask about coffee, the waiter should reply, as naturally as possible, that coffee is served at the counter. The business might not think about having a specific member of staff for making personalised coffees. It is something else worth considering, since every person does whatever they feel best for them.

WAITERS AND TIPS. 203

In catering, customers giving tips to waiters is quite common when they pay the bill. In self-service businesses, the waiter doesn't have that opportunity. The business needs to take this into account, and it is quite common that any tips received in this business are shared between all staff since all participate the food production. Every business has its own way of working. Good sales will come from being in a girl location. I recommend that you work out a certain percentage of commission to give your staff which will help the business to produce and sell more. This will ensure the business earns greater profits. And the waiters can't complain they don't get any tips. Every business has general costs which are covered by the daily or monthly sales. Wouldn't it be logical to give your staff a certain percentage of the total sales? Well, the normal thing is to give a certain percentage of net weekly or monthly profits. What happens in this case? The business covers its costs and gives its staff a percentage of the remaining profits. In catering, sales will clearly be increased by selling a special or unusual dish or dessert, or through quick sales and service. These are all suggestions of course; you could always give commission on total sales.

SHARINGOUT COMMISSION. 204

This percentage and how it is shared out is agreed by the owner in proportion with each staff member's position. You can distribute the money as you see fit. All employees participate in earning profits for the business. If a customer arrives close to closing time, your employees will be more likely to invite them in rather than tell them they're late.
This is something which must be discussed with the head chef to get them involved in sales. Your employees have to know that what they do earns them commission.

THE RELATIONSHIP BETWEEN TABLES AND TRAYS. 205

Ideally, a table with two seats has to be big enough to fit two trays. If we put them together, we have a table for four people, and we can put together as many as necessary. If the trays are too small, the customers won't be able to fit enough on it. Example: if the tray measures 45 cm wide by 35 cm long, the tables would have to be 45 by 70 cm, or a little more. You can decide what is most convenient for you. When a customer comes in alone, he will look for free tables, but there will always be a waiter to tell him where he can sit.
 If we're waiting for a certain group of customers, we can tell the customer who came in alone to sit wherever is best for us. However, occasionally the customers will go where they want to. When we have a building which isn't very big, every centimetre counts. The approximate calculations of a dining room and its size should be worked out to the square metre. In self-service businesses, large trays have more potential when it comes to the till. Some customers only take what they want, but others put food and drink on as long as it fits. Then, if they leave it, that's their problem.
 They've paid for it already. We have to make sure the plates

we use fit well on the trays and aren't too wide. Both plates and bowls of around 22 cm diameter work well. Test for yourself on a table how much space the food - a salad, starter, main course, bread, dessert and drink - takes up on the tray. I'll leave the final decision up to you. If the tables are around ten to twelve centimetres wider than the trays, between the trays, you'll always have that space to put salt, vinegar, bottles, etc., maybe on a shelf. In conclusion, we can have very little space in the premises but the smaller the trays, the fewer the chances of selling. This is something that the organiser has to think about. In à la carte restaurants, you leave more space for everything because they ay more for everything.

CONNECTION BETWEEN COUNTER AND KITCHEN. 206

The sales counter and kitchen should have a direct connection so that everything can be easily restocked when necessary, without leaving the working area. This ensures that the production and sales chain is never stopped.

DINING ROOM CHAIRS AND TABLES. 207

The space a chair takes up is approximately 50x50 cm. Leave a passage between the rows of seats through which people can pass, and so that those sitting down and comfortably sit down and get back up. This is all arranged according to the space available and the kind of business. They are approximate measure to give you some ideas. You should do whatever is most appropriate. There are many types of chairs but they mustn't be folding which could cause problems with your business. We spoke about tables and their size in relation to the trays. The tables can be wooden or metallic and have four legs, without any other bars underneath so that they can be stacked. They must have solid legs so that they don't break easily.

SIZE OF THE PREMISES.   208

This is where the businessman has to do their calculations. Premises which work well are more expensive to rent because they're in better locations. Sometimes, the entrepreneur is the one, with their ideas, who make the business work, even if the premises are not in the perfect spot. In this case, it is experience which is what makes it work. A new entrepreneur can't make mistakes. They need to look for an unarguably good place, and then, once they have more experience, they can decide what they do in the future. Being in the best location costs a lot due to the high rent or loan costs. Getting a good location can be like buying a lottery ticket. That "luck" depends on what you do with the premises. When I talk about a good premises, I'm not referring to the building itself, but rather that there is something key about it. In part one, we talked about these more.

VENTILATION. 209

In this type of business, ventilation is basic, especially in the public areas which will be vital for making sure it is successful. I'm talking to future entrepreneurs here. A place which is too cold or hot will cause customers to leave. Air conditioning is expensive but will end up being profitable as more customers will come back. It heats or cools the premises which is controlled with a thermostat. The air is taken, filtered, heated or cooled and then directed back in. There is a way to change the air in the premises once in a while with the cooler turned off. Install an independent extractor fan in the premises and when you want it to be refreshed, you turn it on. In normal weather, when air conditioning is not necessary, the extractor can ventilate, eliminate odours and smoke, customers are more comfortable and you'll save more electricity. Don't forget that the best treasure a business can have is a customer, so you have to take care of them and make them come back to you.

PUBLIC AND STAFF TOILETS. 210

Every restaurant business is obligated by law to provide toilets to men and women separately. You also have to have toilets and dressing rooms for employees, as mentioned in earlier chapters.

DAYS OFF IN CATERING. 211

Weekends and bank holidays are the ones with most sales. Having days off on these days needs to be done only under certain conditions. Restaurants in industrial areas or other certain areas can be closed on if there are no customers. But in commercial city areas, many people go out to eat and you shouldn't be closed. Experience tells us you'll lose customers. There are many restaurants that never close - certainly the majority. Some are closed on Mondays.
The most profitable thing in the long run is to not close on any day. If you have a couple of extra employees, you could always have some staff off during the week. It all depends on the size of your business. The weekly holidays taken by customers can be on a rota and everyone can have free afternoons when it is their turn. A couple of staff can have the day off and the business will carry on working. We've already explained in the chapter on working extra days how catering businesses often has the opportunity to find

occasional extra workers on holiday days. Luck can be gained through order and discipline at work, well-dressed staff, good, quick service, respectful customer service, and a good quality-price ratio on what we sell. It seems like we're talking as it if were an army. It's not very similar, but it's vital that any business reach their goals. It's very important to work out cost prices upon buying products, so that you charge fair and acceptable prices which still give profits.

Customers can make you as rich or poor as you want. We have luck in our power without knowing it, and we have to find this out to know how to use it. Luck is wonderful, and when it touches us with its magic wand, those that know us say: "How is it that everything you do turns out so well?" You know what? Businessmen play with their cards close to their chest. In business, we're playing to win.

THE OTHER TYPE OF LUCK: GAMBLING. 212

The other thing is that, even gambling a lot, only little money is earned. Luck exists for those running the games. They always win - the odds are on their side. If you want to make easy money, open a bingo hall or a casino - the banker always wins. I remember a book I read about the Blind Association (ONCE) in Spain and the problem their lottery administrators had in handling the more than a billion pesetas that they took in per day. It was a business with huge amounts of money, enormous investments in many varied activities according to this book. And it was all earned through gambling and gamblers. Their "luck" was in setting up the business. They made a business based on luck but they always win.

DISHES AND CUTLERY. 213

Dishes in general should be the usual type. Unbreakable plates, glasses and cups would be the dream of restaurant owners everywhere. So dishes should take this into account and not be so fragile as to chip or break at any touch. It's better if they break than chip. A chipped plate is a sign of poverty. Cutlery can be made of stainless steel because otherwise, when they are only plated with metal, whatever it is, sooner or later it will start wearing off and it'll be another sign of poverty. Glasses must be made of crystal. This kind of business doesn't use tablecloths of napkins made of cloth. They use disposable paper ones. Ones made of cloth are used in à la carte restaurants. You could also have the tables covered in a place mats made of cloth with the glasses on them and no tablecloth. These are a type of tablecloth which only covers the plate and little else. You could also have plastic plates with covers and cups for taking away coffee or other drinks.

THE KITCHEN. 214

In earlier chapters, we saw plenty of ideas about running a restaurant. If you haven't already, there are various chapters on catering you must read. Each one will give you new ideas which will help you make up your mind. Good ventilation is essential in the kitchen. Before buying or renting the premises, it should either already be installed or be agreed that you can install it. A kitchen around 10 or 20 m2 in size could be enough, but it all depends on the general capacity of the business.

An industrial dishwasher, a slicing machine, waste disposal machine, a whisk, a good sink which can be easily managed, large pots and pans, good, strong shelves on which to put clean plates, a cooker with various hobs and an oven (gas should be fine, though the law prohibits gas in basements), a hot water boiler, other shelves, plenty of work surfaces with stainless steel tops, other quick-cook pans, knives, frying pans and other tools, deep-fat fryers, etc. Any other tools which the chef sees necessary. It is essential to have good fridges and freezers. Industrial catering suppliers have everything you'll need, but be careful: they'll try to sell you things you don't need. if they think you can pay.

SELF-SERVICE CAFÉS. 215

This service could be permanently available. Café service is the same as in restaurants, but the food and counters have been transformed into café food and drinks. In the morning, when the customer enters the service passage, he takes a tray which is smaller than the one for meals we saw before and finds pastries, cakes, portions of butter, jam, sandwiches and a multitude of other foods which sell at that time Portions of cake and anything else you find appealing, French toast, boiled eggs, various sandwiches, other vegetables, tapas, hot meals and others to be heated in the microwave. Anything which could be served at breakfast and between main meals will be on individual plates.

The customer should take cutlery and paper napkins as they want. We can also sell drinks, natural juices and others, ¼- and ½-litre bottles of wine and milk-based drinks. Ice cubes. When they have what they want, before getting to the till, there will be a coffee machine, a stand with alcohol and a waiter to serve them what they want more quickly. This will be close to the till so that the coffee has less time to cool down before getting to the table.

These explanations might be repetitive and lengthy, but if they weren't, how would you learn from my experience to be successful? At meal times, you should take away some of the pastries and replace them with other light foods, such as vegetables, soup, pulses, croquettes, meat in sauce, pork, chicken or beef pies, a fish pie with the bones taken out, etc., which can be heated in the microwave when ordered. Later, these foods can be taken away and we go back to the standard sandwiches and pastries. At night, at dinner time, we'll put the food out again, and then close the business when convenient. Closing time should come at whatever time is suitable. We have already discussed how we can keep different foods for the next day.

CHAPTER 6 - 216

RESTAURANTS FOR BANQUETS, WEDDINGS, COMMUNIONS AND SO ON. 217

A normal restaurant can serve banquets as long as it has enough space. Quite a large building is necessary in these cases since the size dictates the services that can be offered. Any wedding may have one, two or three hundred, or even more, guests. You never know. When we serve banquets, it's no longer necessary to have a building in a central location. It may be wherever is comfortable and has good parking, since the capacity of the building is more important than the location. Having said that, it's still better, if possible, to have the location not too far from the city centre. Perhaps, on the main roads leading to or from a city. I remember a small pub on a side street whose owner had served banquets in the past. He rented a couple of large premises across the street from his pub and dedicated them to banquets. When he didn't have banquets, he kept them closed. He fitted them with the furnishings necessary for that service. Toilets and kitchen fitted as we've already seen. He advertised for more customers. When they came, he'd show them the dining room only be crossing the street. For several years, he served banquets for weddings and communions

LARGE-SCALE BANQUETS. 218

This businessman I mentioned was clever. His experience helped him to start a new business with his speciality. I was once invited to a banquet at his place. It is located near a general main road, about ten kilometres from the city of Zaragoza. Some turned up in hired cars and others went in coaches hired by the same company that serves the banquets, from the church or place where the marriage took place to the restaurant, and at the end, they were taken back, making all the trips necessary. Upon arrival, there is a large private car park. It's a newly-constructed building made for this business. When you go in, there is a greeter, in a wide passage, some decorations on the walls, good lights and a few gardens around about. Walking along the corridors, we saw doors leading to different-sized private dining rooms. There was a small room with cribs for babies, a kind of nursery for the young children brought by the guests. This business works exclusively with banquets for weddings and other events, apart from other special parties, which can be on any day of the week. In general, wedding banquets are the most frequent, taking place on Fridays, Saturdays and Sundays, and a few other holidays. If you've never worked with banquets before, you'll never be able to image the size of the business. You may end up going one or two thousand meals to diners, or even more. Well, I'm not going to talk about numbers here. If you have enough space, it will be a very busy trade.

EXAMPLE OF ECONOMIC CALCULATIONS DURING BANQUETS. 219

I'm doing these calculations off the top of my head - we can never be absolutely certain. I just want to give you an idea of the potential in this business. If we have a business with three dining rooms in which 600 guests can fit, and we half-fill the rooms, we'll have three hundred people per week. Four weeks would be 1,200 per month. If we imagine an average of 50 euros per service, as an average, or even more, the money we take per month will be 60,000, which multiplied by 12 months, gives 720,000 euros. This is an approximate idea of the money we could get. Speaking of this kind of business, I think it's difficult for a businessman to start here with little money. But it could be a goal to aim for if you want to go far. This sample business could be a sign where we could set our goals. The taxes for this kind of business are the same as a normal restaurant. Other taxes are paid according to the size and location, as with any other business.

CUSTOMER OPPORTUNITIES. 220

Banquet service is very demanding. Churches only marry at weekends. Registry offices or courts may be available on other days, but couples always choose weekend for their guests' convenience. Banquets, therefore, are usually held on Fridays, Saturdays and Sundays.
This is a benefit because, since we are open for fewer days, all these restaurants are booked a long time in advance. When you start this type of business, after a short time, you will have agreed so many dates for banquets that before you realise it, you'll have your diary full of bookings with a lot of notice in advance.

CUSTOMERS VISITING LOOKING FOR A FREE DAY TO - HAVE A BANQUET. 221

When a customer turns up to book a banquet at a restaurant, there will already be prepared menus of different types and prices. Some won't be interested and won't come back and some will. Some will spend time thinking about it and, when they come back, that day they wanted is now busy. When they first visit, show them the dining room, explain what you provide and tell them how wonderful your service is.
If they seem interested, invite them to have something to drink while you explain how it works and what you offer, such as a ball with a free bar, and so on. The idea is to fill the customer's head with how wonderful your place is and

convince them it's the place they're looking for. We have to be salespeople until the end of our days.

PAYING FOR THE BANQUET. 222

On booking a banquet, the customer has to be told the payment conditions clearly. You should have a standard contract prepared to explain the menu price per head. The extra services also need to have the price agreed, as well as the method of payment. When this agreement is made, even if there are months to go until the party, the customer should pay thirty percent of the total cost as a deposit. Another forty percent will be charged thirty days before the banquet date. When this date arrives, if they haven't come to pay the second payment, call them to remind them. The remaining cost will be paid on the day of the banquet. The total bill or invoice will be given after the banquet in case there are any other unforeseen costs which crop up which haven't been paid for.
Some guests will prefer some other food for whatever reason. You should give it to them without charging extra. Other requests will be clearly extra costs outside of the agreed menu. In this case, speak to the person who booked the banquet, and if they agree to pay the extra, give them what they ask for. Some customers may otherwise ask for something and the one who pays the bill may not agree with this. When the guests are seated and eating, count the number of guests twice so as not to make a mistake with the number of people who attended. The final bill should have an itemised list of what is being charged.
In the standard contract, at the bottom, in fine print, you will include the terms and conditions. If they want to cancel the banquet a short time after booking, charge a moderate fee. If the cancellation is only a few days before the banquet, there may be no other chance of getting another customer on that day. In this case, the fee charged will be higher, since your

losses will be considerable if no-one comes on that day. It must be clearly written in the contract that the initial deposit will be lost, or whatever we find most convenient. This should be done by a lawyer. When talking about guests who didn't turn up, you should charge 10% of whatever food they were going to have. If, on the other hand, the number of guests is higher than expected, charge the price for every one of the ones that came with any other supplementary charges. If the business is in charge of name cards written at each seat, these should also be charged for. You could also charge an extra 10% on the cost of the menu for those who want to have a second dessert. To the total cost, you will add the corresponding VAT. This must all be written in the contract so that the customer knows exactly what they have to pay. All this relevant information can be summarised at the bottom of the contract. Remember, whatever is written and signed is important.

THE MEANS OF PAYMENT. 223

If a customer decides to make the booking and gives you a cheque, this can be put in the bank or cashed. If you're a customer of that bank, you may be interested in that customer's banking reports in case they pay you with cheques. You can choose whether or not to accept a cheque for the second payment. The third and final payment must be made in cash or a guaranteed cheque, along with the rest of the unforeseen costs. The ideal thing is to have all cheques guaranteed by the respective banks. Cases in which people leave without paying are not common. However, getting this third payment is the

most important. This isn't mistrust, it's simply being sure. It's vital to get this final payment before all the guests leave. If anything goes wrong or you trust someone and it goes wrong, don't blame me. Anyway, things are not so serious: at weddings, people are usually proud and will pay before the wedding, but... you never know.

THE DISCO. 224

Dining rooms often have a long area which can be used as a dance floor. Customers usually prefer private areas for their guests. You should bear in mind that no more than 20% of the guests will get up onto the dance floor. With this in mind, you can work out about how much space you'll need. When giving the price per meal per person, you can also offer a disco for afterwards. This has an extra price not included in the menu. It includes free bar during the music, both for those dancing and those sitting. Make it clear that this refers to normal drinks. If they ask for a bottle of champagne or cava, this will be extra. This is just a suggestion, but it's something which could make the final bill look a lot more attractive to the business. Many people will drink nothing while others have drink after drink.

You can calculate the cost of the free bar at about one drink per guest. The disco has to be confirmed when making the first payment. At this time, you should give them a bill for the total in which it shows the corresponding prices for the meals, disco, decorations, name cards, etc. During the disco, you should have a mini bar and a bartender to serve the guests.......

EXAMPLE OF A WEDDING MEAL. 225

Examples of .... Menu no. 10

(1st course) Various hors d'oeuvres, hot and cold, consisting of ham, salad, boiled egg, cooked prawns, pasties and croquettes, etc.

(2nd course)Baked sea bass with a vegetable garnish. (3rd course)Beef steak in sauce and peas. Wedding Cake. Ice-cream, cava, selected wines, coffee and spirits. Price €80 plus VAT (it's an example, since the prices will be related to the quality), and the corresponding prices for the season and country. We have to remember that this is to have an idea, and set the price correctly for us. At the end of the menus, it could say the following:

Extras for the big occasion.

Menu cards and floral decorations: 10% extra. 5% discount per meal without spirits. 5% discount per meal without cava. For each guest that doesn't come, we charge 10% of the price of their meal. (It could also say at the end of the orders which the person hands in: "Floral decorations and personalised cards at your choice. Menu combinations can be modified. Please don't hesitate in letting us know what you'd like".) It's good to have samples of the table cards with the menus so that the customer can choose one they'd like. They will tell you what they want the card to say as well as telling us the menu they want.

ABOUT MUSIC AND DANCING AT THE BANQUET. 226

It's common to have two musicians with instruments like piano or organ, and so on. I've also seen some places which giant screens in which you can see an orchestra playing modern songs. It's all a question of having the right songs and music equipment. The times the music is played should be decided in advance. The normal thing is that the meals and dancing together should be no longer than four hours. If the meals are served at two in the afternoon, the disco should be finished by six or very little after, since you have to get the tables ready for the following banquet. If it were up to the guests, they may stay all day and end up mixing with the next party.

Those that start eating at nine at night must be finished by half past one, or two in the morning. Staff have to know in advance when their working day finished, though in catering, it's all relative. In such cases, the extra waiters end their day when the plates are taken away, and the coffee and spirits are served. The regular waiters stay for any extras and to control the services. Sometimes, one or two for a banquet is enough. As regards the price of the disco, if they are musicians, you should charge double what you pay them because there are always other costs.

For example: if we have a banquet with a hundred people, we'll charge a hundred drinks at the bar plus the cost of the musicians. Then you have the extras that don't come into the agreement. The final agreed price would be the price of the disco with free bar plus the cost of the menus. This is all approximate of course - we will pay attention to the circumstances and current prices.

TOILETS AT BANQUETS. 227

The technician who works on the project will decide the amount of space. It should be related to the capacity of the building, as with the staff toilets and dressing rooms. More information in the first chapters. Modern custom is to have obligatory disabled toilets, if not by law. The corresponding department in your town hall or council will tell you the laws on these.

THE KITCHEN FOR BANQUETS.   228

They must be big enough to prepare all the food necessary. Everything which has been arranged ahead of time will always turn out fine, since various banquets may occur at the same time. When you tak charge of a wedding, you already have to be thinking about the next one. One at two in the afternoon and the other at two-thirty. You have to have the appropriate cookers, ovens and grills. When the quantity of guests is high, the kitchen tools and amount of food need to be equally big. A general example: if we have various banquets at midday, and there are main courses with steaks and others with fish, they should be made on the same day in advance and kept warm for these cases. If you put on the menus: "juicy grilled lamb" or "juicy grilled sirloin steak with such-and-such sauce", or any other phrase which may tell them that it will be juicy, we have to make sure that it is, even if it takes longer to make. They will be hot and you can put on some of their hot juices when you serve them. These are matters for the kitchen, which the entrepreneur will find out in time.

When you are learning things on the spot, anything is difficult. Don't forget what I said earlier: the job will teach us enough. The most difficult thing in this business is having the money or credit necessary, and finding the ideal place. The rest, with the help of an expert, is a piece of cake.

THE KITCHEN HAS TO WORK LIKE A FACTORY. 229

When a banquet is booked, the customer has to know that the business works better if everyone has the same meal. This job of convincing the customer about the food is something which is more easily done by someone who has experience or good training in doing so. It is much easier for the head chef and the kitchen staff in general if all customers have the same food. It's very difficult for every meal to be exactly the same, but that's the objective. This is a suggestion but with good organisation, nothing is difficult. We have to have enough space, open shelves, easy access to all tools and equipment needed by anyone. If we need two hundred plates of hors d'oeuvres, or five hundred or more, we can't have just one person who makes one plate, then another and another. One employee puts a slice of ham on every plate and then another puts all the croquettes, and so on.

This is done as a series with all the people necessary. Jobs which are well-organised in a series like this will be all the same and done more quickly. The plate stands or shelves for prepared meals are very important also since making this number of dishes will take up a lot of space.

THE SAME WAITERS FOR THE SAME BANQUETS. 230

Something else to keep thinking about. Don't be worried by the number of people. Every dining room can have a waiter and helper, who will make sure everything is in order and everything is in its place. Bread and drinks which aren't cold will be on the tables. The head waiter (in charge of all service in general) is the one who decides which dining room is served first. He knows the meals in each banquet and will decide for both the kitchen and waiters when and to whom to serve

The head chef and head waiter are vital to get the business working. When the waiter says to the chef: "Serve the first dish to dining room number one". At that moment, the kitchen staff and waiters become robots. All available waiters take the first dishes to that dining room. If they are hors d'oeuvres, any fried food will be put on the plates of cold food already prepared a little before the service begins. For second courses, one person brings clean plates, another puts on the meat or fish, others add the garnishes, etc., the waiters gradually take those dishes, and after a little while, the service is finished. Some adult may say that he is on a diet, so we can be nice and serve him vegetables with boiled fish or whatever else, without needing to charge more as we've already discussed. The head waiter and head chef have already discussed what will happen next, and they'll start taking the food out to dining room number two. Immediately after, they'll start with number three. Very soon, the first dining room will have finished, and the waiters will start clearing away the plates. Then the second courses will come, and so on. You mustn't forget that the food is first served to the bridge and groom. If it is a long table and they are in the centre, serve them first and then the ones next to them.

DESSERTS CHAMPAGNE OR CAVA. 231

Once the second course plates have been taken away, the wedding cake is brought. It's a custom to have a large knife which isn't very sharp for the bride and groom to cut the cake first. Serve the bride and groom their slice first and then rest will be taken back to the kitchen to be divided for the rest of the guests. It can be done in the dining room, but in the kitchen is better. Then the cava or champagne is taken to the table. Work it out at approximately one bottle for every four people and serve half glasses for everyone. When everyone has been served, the waiters will go around again and give more cava to anyone who wants it. You can also leave opened, half-full bottles on each table so they can serve themselves. These calculations are approximate, and you will have put in the price whatever you think is best. Someone may order more champagne, which is no problem until the agreed number of bottles have been served. If any guest orders anything expensive which wasn't agreed in the original price, the person who made the booking will make the decision on whether to allow it since it will need to be charged as an extra. The head table, with the bride, groom and their families, will have priority for everything.

COFFEE SERVICE. 232

Some waiters will bring cups for coffee, while others have jugs of milk and hot coffee, sugar, decaffeinated coffee bags, hot water and tea bags, or other infusions. The waiter only needs to ask: "Black? Or white?" There won't be many people who have infusions but it's better to avoid going back to the kitchen. Another waiter may have two or three bottles of spirits and serve drinks after the coffee to anyone who asks. Afterwards, some may ask for a little more or some water. If any other drink is ordered, we serve it because it's included. Some people will be difficult and keep ordering. We serve them but not too often. When we work out the prices to give each menu, we calculate an average, since many people won't have any alcohol while others will have a lot. It all balances out. The aim is to serve each guest as quickly as possible while maintaining good customer service. If there are only six permanent waiters, you may need another ten or however many extra. These waiters are hired only for such banquets.

PERMANENT EMPLOYEES. 233

You may employee only enough permanent employees for the business to run normally at all times, and then hire extras for banquets. The head chef and kitchen staff are usually permanent. The number of employees is not fixed; it all depends on the size of the business. You may have a restaurant with regular daily customers as well as serving banquets, so you will need some permanent staff for that. When a business is solely dedicated to banquets, half of the days of the week can be half-days for organising the business and other essentials. The key days will be a little longer... And we come back to the same chorus: the job teaches you, and practice makes you a master. Employees can have days off because they work more hours at weekends. In their contract, employees will have different working times set in accordance with the needs of the business. Once you have the building and know its capacity, it's easy to work out how many staff are needed.

Staff will never be a problem. There are a lot of waiters available for various motives, whether they are students or work in other trade who also work at weekends as waiters to earn more. Even if they are not professionals, they learn quickly since this job is a routine which is learned quickly. There are also catering professionals or work in other jobs and work extra at weekends. In the chapter on extra jobs, I explain how to find and pay these extra workers who usually have permanent jobs in other companies. It is just another job. It may look difficult but it isn't once you practice a bit. However, if you think that you can cook without being a professional, you're wrong. You have a look for an efficient chef with good experience.

BUILDING AND DINING TABLES. 234

There are some buildings of this type which have so much space that they have curtains or screens which can be moved and used to separate dining rooms according to the needs of the moment. In this way, you can have various services at the same time, especially communions which usually don't have so many guests as weddings.

MULTIPLE TABLES.   235

When we have normal restaurants, it's very common to have table tops to put tables together and improvise long tables. These are the same width as the normal tables and are supported by solid trestles or on tables at each end of the top. In this way, you can make tables as long as you want them, at which guests can sit on both side. It's also very common to have round tables at which there are six, eight or ten spaces. You have to arrange these as you see fit with the space and furniture available. The restaurants dedicated exclusively to banquets usually have the appropriate furniture in advance which, in general, are round tables and a long one for the bride and groom's families, facing the guests.

VENTILATION.   236

This kind of business works in all seasons. So it's necessary to have hot and cold air conditioning, so the room will always be comfortable. You absolutely need a comfortable atmosphere since many guests may turn out to be future brides and grooms, and therefore customers. If only one guest is unhappy, it may produce a bad campaign against our company. We have to do all we can to give the best service, and actually be the best. Of course, we also have to charge for everything. Winning over customers for them to come back in the future won't cost us any more money but it will help us in the future. Working harder and being better will help to make us rich, while stinginess brings poverty. The choice is in your hands. If we have good food and customer service at normal prices, that will be enough for others to come back in the future.

STAFF UNIFORM.   237

Waiters and waitresses must always look perfect. The uniform has to be the classic black jacket, trousers or skirt, black shoes, white shirt and a tie or bow-tie. If the weather is warm, we can be a little lenient, for example, a waistcoat instead of a jacket.
The image of the business is given by the staff, their manners and cleanliness, since this is what the guests remember. This may have good or bad consequences for the business. If the customer service is good but the food is bad, or vice versa, this will be notices straight away. How can we avoid this? Easy: be the best at everything we do. Even if we're not the best, we'll always be excellent. The manager can't hesitate in telling his staff about their appearance, personal hygiene or respect towards any person, regardless of how they appear. Appearances can be deceiving, and it's easy to be wrong.

.OTHER RECOMMENDATIONS.   238

 If one of your employees ever breaks any of the house rules, they must be sacked immediately. They may create problems and not give a good impression to the business. Both good and bad behaviour is contagious. In this trade, there needs to be a good understanding between those in charge and those who obey, and no-one can come and change the rules. If discipline and order is implemented from the first day, people who won't adapt will leave. Remember, at the same time, that being nice to people is much better than otherwise. All businesses work well with steel fists and velvet gloves. It's always a good idea to have all managers or heads directing employees with your orders. My friend, starting a restaurant of this type is neither easier nor more difficult than any other business. If you've worked in this trade before, I'm sure that you already know half of what you read here. There will be many other things in this trade which are purely business matters which you never knew before but now you do, right? An entrepreneur who has never worked in this business before has to realise that it's just another business, and if you've read the previous pages, you'll know what to do to achieve success in anything you do. Never forget that's it's just another business. But it's one of the good ones.

PLACES WHERE THESE BUSINESS WORK WELL. 239

As I explained, the important thing is the amount of space. The idea thing is to have an industrial premises on a busy road, not far from a town or city or other population hub, and that you are near an industrial area so that you have plenty of space for car parking. The advantage is that we can have a normal daily restaurant starting with breakfasts. Don't worry if this seems like a lot of work. You'll have to have employees through necessity, and therefore you won't be so much of a slave as if you have one of those jobs in other companies you can't leave.

These businesses are planned so that by working with good upper management or managers who take charge of the staff, and when one isn't there, there'll be another. Our business is assured by the daily customers, and with banquets added, it'll be a super-business. Starting a.

business with this knowledge is squaring the circle. nother possibility, if there is no industrial park which will help us out, is to have a motorway restaurant weekends. The entrepreneur mustn't be put off by the amount of work going into this business, since most of it for him is organising it. Then, with the help of staff, everything keeps rolling along, and you may even have time for fishing, playing tennis or whatever else you enjoy. But the truth is that you will have created your own business.

ABOUT RENTING OR BUYING AN INDUSTRIAL PREMISES. 240

It's good to have it at a crossroads or a main road near a city, or a building with space for gardens and parking. The ideal thing is to buy and have it paid off in thirty years. It will be partly tax-deductible. If the idea is to rent, the contract should be done by a good lawyer and should include the rights to buy within a reasonable deadline. Otherwise, you may be working only to lose it all someday. If you don't know how this works, I'll give you a brief explanation. The right to buying a rented building.

 (A lawyer is important for <u>expressing this in a contract when the rental is agreed.) Example of a</u> contract: "This building and the adjoining car park are worth (what they are worth). They are being rented for (the amount of money agreed per month. There is a right to buy them after three or five years (or whatever)." The owner will give this period of time to the tenant to decide if they want to buy it. The money paid through rental is discounted from the total value to pay for the house. This is delicate and has to be done with the knowledge and assurance of an expert lawyer. When the entrepreneur discovers that the payment of a mortgage can be done with the payment of the rent, he understands it quite well. He gets a loan over various years and pays back the loan with the money recovered from what was paid in rent. This is one possibility of buying, which is the best way of doing business in the future. Always remember that the good path, or the "lucky path", is the one the entrepreneur takes. That's what I say "you have to think about every possibility before starting any type of business".

MENUS FOR BANQUETS WHEN "STARTING OUT" 241

Send a person you trust to various restaurants of this type saying that you're looking for a restaurant for a wedding and you need menus and prices (which will be easy). When you have a business of the type we're talking about, you'll give out lots of menus and you'll never hear back from them. With these menus as ideas, you can create your own, either modifying or creating from scratch, but they'll all give you ideas about what you can offer. When you have decided on the menus, send them to a printing shop with the outline of what you want. Printing shops always have specialised staff for these types of thing who do them very well. Everything matters to the customer: the image of your business, what you offer, and the prices and types of food. A few weeks of having this business will be more than enough to invent dishes and menus you like. If you find a good, experienced cook, he can help invent dishes, but never with the prices. That's something for the business.

COST CALCULATIONS. 242

If you've never done this before, I'll explain how you have to proceed. You'll be able to make any business succeed with what you read in this book together with professional and trained staff. If you don't know how much money a portion of sirloin or fillet steak, or a particular type of fish costs, you just need to tell the cook to cut a kilo of meat into portions for a meal or banquet, count the pieces and find out the cost. Divide the cost of a kilo over the number of pieces you get and you'll know the price of each one.
The businessman must know what every portion of everything used in the business costs so that they can work out the sale price. If you want to be more methodical, get

some small scales and weigh everything when it is raw. You'll quickly find out the cost of everything. Write it down; don't trust your memory. If you want to work out the cost of a meal, add together the cost of each item and then add the cost of every material used. If this is for a normal restaurant, multiply it by three or four. If it's a banquet, by even more, since it's a special service in which you need bigger and better services and facilities. Even so, I'll say it again; you need to get menus from other restaurants which will tell you what is best for you. I know of one restaurant which, once the banquet has been booked and the first payment made, invites the bride and groom to a meal which is similar to the one on the wedding day. This is publicity, done only if the money is worth it. Being generous doesn't mean giving away everything you have. Remember that no-one every got rich by giving.

FOOD STORAGE. 243

It's important to have a well-controlled store, with plenty of shelves and a good freezer, since a lot of the food you use will be kept frozen. When we talk about large services, you can't go looking for prices at the moment you need them. You need to get stock months in advance. Anticipation in everything is vital, as should be clear by now. As the saying goes: forewarned is forearmed. There has to be someone in charge of stock control who always knows what there is and what needs to be restocked.

If all employees go in and take stock out without control, the day may arrive that whatever you need isn't there, and it won't be anyone's fault. For that reason, a stock supervisor is essential. He writes down whatever goes in and comes out, and he'll always know what is in each fridge, freezer or on each shelf. You can even control the stock if there are rats!

Large businesses will bring bigger profits, and there will always be some leaks through cracks (they are sometimes inevitable), but if you don't control the stock, these cracks get bigger and bigger. A business guru once told me: "Stock control must never be shared between various people, because you'll never know who was responsible for the problems!" In order to start this kind of business, you should do everything possible, even selling the shirt off your back, because the next ones you buy will be made of silk.Note: Needless to say, in a banquet meal, cutlery and glasses should be complete and of the best quality, as well as fabric tablecloths and napkins. If this business is run with the help of a true professional, as it must be, he will be the best source of advice for the job and necessary materials.

THE NEED FOR PUBLICITY. 244

As we already know, publicity is essential for any business to grow. In this case specifically, it's even more important to cover the whole area since many people will come long distances. These costs will be compensated for by the profits made. Publicity, to be effective, should be left to an agency who will deal with this well.

CHAPTER 7   245

ALL-YOU-CAN-EAT BUFFETS.   246

All-you-can-eat buffets are quite normal in many hotels. It consists of customers choosing the food that they want and taking it to their table. The basic facilities and service is similar to any other restaurant that we've seen in other chapters.

Installing an all-you-can-eat buffet. The containers which hold the food that the customers can take are similar to those in self-service, though with one difference. They can be in a separate counter at one side of the premises, though still should be connected to the kitchen through the part opposite the side where customers take the food. They are designed to keep food either hot or cold. You can have them installed at your convenience but the most practical ones are those connected to the kitchen. Some have the form of an island surrounded by trays with food on.

HOW THE BUSINESS WORKS.   247

The containers are available for customers to serve themselves. They have to be not too large or deep, because it's not a good idea to have too much of one food. On the other hand, it's good to have a lot of variety to increase sales. Remember always to think as a customer because if we think plates, you can have stews, types of soup, mashed potato, grilled meat, fish, etc... There are many varieties of cold food you can offer, such as tuna, chicken or fish salads, vinaigrettes, tinned fish, various types of eggs, cheeses and meats of various types. When I talk about salads, you can have separate trays of sliced carrot, lettuce, onion, tomato and any other product used to make salads. Besides being attractive, it's good for the customers to make their own food, and they are also easy to keep. Any cook knows a lot on this topic, but you don't need to be happy with just this.

Visit different types of restaurants of this type and you'll see different ways to distribute the food and work the business. Take note and decide which foods are most popular. You can also use it to get a good idea of the food containers you'll need. A good place to go is to hotel dining rooms in summer and self-service restaurants in cities. In terms of desserts, you can have various types of fruit in syrup, flans, various flavours of ice-cream and a mixture of pastries or cakes. In these restaurants, the food is usually good quality at medium cost.

You can't use high-cost food because the prices are usually higher than those in a popular menu. In hotels, the quality is related to the price and category of the hotel, apart from those which usually have pensioners which have prices agreed ahead of time and whose food is similar to the popular restaurants.

You have to realise that you'll use a lot of food. Some places have a sign advising customers only to put the food on their plate that they actually want to eat.

DRINKS. 248

On entering the dining area, there should be a sign which says the price of the food, excluding drinks. In general, drinks are charged for separately and are not included in the cost of the all-you-can-eat food. You can work out what cost is convenient for you ahead of time. Some places have a notepad where they note down what you drink when you order it. This is for better control and means that only the till is involved with the money. You can also charge for the food when the person enters, and when they need a drink, they go to a counter and pay the staff there. This counter can also sell coffee and spirits which are also not included with the food. When you go to one of these businesses, I'm sure you'll copy whatever you feel is best. If a customer asks for tap water and not mineral which is charged, serve them water from the tap, without being cold. It's the only way that they'll go for drinks they have to pay for. These are ideas that you can modify if you want. You could also give them some ice.

SUITABLE FURNITURE.   249

It's common to have furniture and display windows for food as we've seen in other chapters. Others for desserts, cutlery, bread, napkins, plates, etc. There should also be a table on which customers can leave their dirty plates and take other clean ones. A member of staff should watch over this and make sure the plates don't stack up too high. They can put any waste food in an appropriate container, put more food which is running low, and make sure the cutlery doesn't go in with the wasted food. Tables don't need to be so big as in banquets since a single person may sit at a table for four people.

CUSTOMERS AT AN ALL-YOU-CAN-EAT BUFFET.   250

Most customers will eat a little of lots of foods, which others only have a few. Portions of dessert have to be small. Customers will make various trips until they are full. I've also seen in some places with flans on trays on which the customers could serve themselves whatever slice they wanted. A lot of food is eaten according to the number of customers. It's not one of the best recommended businesses although there is no fixed rule. There are some which are so well-organised that they could be worth it.

In order to be profitable, you need a lot of customers. I know some of the largest Spanish businesses of this type, spread over various provinces, ended up closing this service. Why? I'm sure that it was bad business because of the amounts of food they lost without being controlled. I, as a businessman, prefer self-service where they pay for what they eat, unless they are hotels which have other profits from people staying and so on.

WHERE TO SET UP THIS TYPE OF BUSINESS. 251

They are set up in areas with lots of people since these pre-prepared foods need to have plenty of customers. The rest of the facilities are similar to other normal restaurants. Kitchens, toilets, ventilation and so on. The price can be quite tricky: if it's expensive, you won't sell a lot, and if it's cheap, you won't make money. In this case, the owner has to use their intelligence. Cold plates are the most common, as I've already explained. Massive sales are found in large cities and busy tourist spots.

DELIVERING FOOD TO HOMES OR UNDER CONTRACT TO OTHER CUSTOMERS. 252

This is the delivery of cooked food to customers, whether they are factories, schools or other businesses. This is becoming more accepted every day by businesses, and these specialised businesses should be paid quite well. You have to go look for customers in this case. This is something which a person who is a good salesman has to do. In the contract you have with the company, you have to specify the type of food, amount of bread and dessert, and the price for each meal and breakfast. You should also specify the approximate time the food will arrive.

WHEN SHOULD I GIVE THEM THE BILL TO PAY? 253

In schools, factories and so on, the charge could be weekly or fortnightly from the date the service begins. The portions needed for each day will be agreed in the contract, apart from if the company wants something different on a certain day more or less, which should be specified to the supplier the day before its service. Food is served in special containers, closed to ensure the food stays hot. Any other requests will be charged for when they are delivered.

CATERING SERVICE TO BUSINESSES. 254

The business or school itself will be in charge of distributing the food to each customer. The pot or pans used are collected the next day when delivering the food for that day. Customers give back these pots perfectly clean. Later, the business will deep-clean them with soap and hot water. The customers, whether they are factories, schools or any others, will receive a note telling them the meals they will receive in the next fortnight.

<u>Meals and their suitability.</u> Meals delivered to factory workers will usually be heavier meals. The start will be a large portion of stew or salad of any type. The main course, normal and of the type we talked about for popular restaurants. The full meal may consist of a starter and main, bread, a drink and a dessert.

CATERING SERVICE TO SCHOOLS. 255

For schools, bear in mind that eating vegetables is good for young people, but if they throw away lots of them because they don't eat them, that won't be good either. The best thing is to serve rice, pasta, beans, croquettes and any other easily-chewable food. If you serve fish, you have to remove all the bones and make sure that all the food is tasty. Other suitable dishes are meat, pies or pasties, maybe with some sauce. The meals consist of a salad or other starter, a main, bread, dessert and a drink. When the kids get home, the majority of their mothers will ask what they've eaten. We have to provide a good variety of food so they don't protest. Everything has to be supplied as in the contract, such as loaves of bread which the business can slice, or individual buns will have a higher cost.

THE DELIVERY VAN. 256

You have to think of the means of transport which could be a delivery van, fitted with fixed shelves on which you can place the trays of food. The driver should have clearly noted what needs to be delivered to each place. When delivering the food, the person who receives it has to sign a delivery note. The driver will then collect the pots from the previous day. This driver will be another employee in our company who, once they have finished the deliveries, helps with other jobs. In general, only breakfast and lunch is served with these companies.

THE KITCHEN. 257

These are different from those of a normal restaurant. There are more powerful cookers with more hobs, and the pans are mostly fast-cook, industrial ones. The equipment used in this kitchen are fridges, freezers and various others we've already talked about. Of course, the kitchen has to be big enough for this type of business. Always bear in mind that this is a food factory.

STOREROOM. 258

The storeroom has to bigger than a normal restaurant which holds enough non-perishable stock. The food is served wholesale and should be bought in the same way. There will be fridges and freezers big enough to hold this.

KITCHEN STAFF. 259

There should always be a head cook with enough experience to get good value for money who has the necessary helpers. At the end of the day, the kitchen will be completely clean and the business will work better.

ECONOMIC CALCULATIONS. 260

These should never be in the hands of the cooks. They are there to cook. The owner is there to calculate. We've already seen the theory of the costs of food. An adult needs a hundred grams of dry pulses for a portion, while kids need less. The type of food served is the popular type. Customers look a lot at the prices so they have to be very cost-effective if we want to sell while earning money and customers.

LOCATION FOR A CATERING BUSINESS. 261

The best thing is a building in an industrial park. I remember having visited a business of this type in which, besides delivering food to factories and school, they served good-price meals to businesses in the same park in a kind of basic dining room. It was made with long tables with many places and wooden benches. It didn't look at all like a restaurant and it was very simple; they only had a starter and main course (without any changes), water or wine and a dessert of fruit or something similar. The food was served from a pot or pan directly to the customer at the table (like in a family). When entering, you had to pay the corresponding fixed price. There was no coffee or any extras. A cheap price and a service to match.

Could we put another type of service? This is a very particular case, maybe even unique. Other ideas are left up to the entrepreneur. The other ways that it could work in an industrial park depend on the number of businesses and customers. Industrial parks come in many types and the work itself will teach us how we need to move forward. Some businesses could work serving first and second courses, or even as self-service.

General facilities. They will be like any other type of business of this type. As explained, there will be a toilet for gentlemen and other for women, relatively simple.

OTHER PRODUCTS MADE IN CATERING BUSINESSES.- 262

Traditional *churros*. This is a traditional Spanish product, a long, thin strip of fried dough, though in some areas, the tradition is being lost, though some places always keep the custom, like in cafés. The format and presentation of these depend on each region. In Madrid, they are usually made in the shape of a ribbon. In other areas such as Aragón or Catalonia, they are in slices of ten or twelve centimetres. Others include ribbons or spirals, or others taking up the whole frying pan and then cut into slices. The most profitable, because they are the quickest to make, are those cut with scissors as they come out of the machine which then go straight into a frying pan. They are regularly sold in different areas of any town or city in fairs and markets. At key times of the day, their shops become factories.

The secret to continuous production is a good cooker and

large frying pans so that the oil doesn't cool down. Ah, and the cooker should be gas or electric which are easy to maintain.

HOT CHOCOLATE WITH *CHURROS* AND THEIR TRADITIONS. 263

Drinking hot chocolate with *churros* has been a tradition on Sundays and bank holidays at breakfast or for snacks for many years. Today, thanks to various innovations and the amount of products available to the market, this custom is being lost. However, there are now machines in cafés and pubs which can make *churros* themselves, so the tradition is not completely lost
.
INSTALLING THESE MACHINES. 264

In spite of the various electric machines which have been built, the traditional manual ones still exist and are the ones that you usually see at any large fair. Mobile *churro* machines are fixed to the side of the oven, right next to the frying pan.

The *churros* can be made to go directly into the middle of the frying pan or separately. In bars, bakers' or cafés, the machine can be attached to a wall so that it can also be put directly into a frying pan or separate. If you put it in a wall, there's a way to be safe. Make the holes on the wall where you'll put the machine. You have to put pieces of iron in the wall and cover them with mortar, as a builder would say. Since pushing to get the inside of the wall to come out creates a lot of pressure, the plaster mixes with hot water. Cover the hole with the machine and it will set like marble. Another thing that not even builders are taught.

CHURRO FRYING PANS. 265

In these businesses, pubs, hotels and so on, the frying pan is usually stainless steel with electric resistors at the bottom. These are covered in oil and plugged in to the mains. The ones in fairs are larger to ensure continuous frying. These use gas heaters which can be turned up or down depending on the moment.

RECIPE FOR THIN *CHURRO* DOUGH, MADE MANUALLY. 266

The basic recipe: a kilo of flour, a litre and a half of water, a pinch of salt dissolved in the water. Heat the flour and then sieve it, since if the *churro* isn't moist, it will be hard or lumpy, and have to be thrown away. The container holding the flour has to be big enough since it has to be poured into boiling water. The secret to this dough is to make the mixture of water and flour as quickly as possible, quickly combining the two to make even the slightest trace of water disappear. When touching the mixture with the hand, it shouldn't be sticky. The flour has to be really warm when mixed so that it combines more quickly. This is done quickly once the water and flour are mixed. The container needs to be held still, while a large wooden spoon or something similar is used to mix the two. (Be careful that the mixture doesn't burn.) You should get good dough from this.

 The wet parts at the sides of the container which wouldn't mix are taken out and thrown away. If they are mixed afterwards, the mixture may go bad. Once the dough is made, place a cloth which has been dampened with oil over the dough. Hard parts may form on the surface of the dough after some time, and these should be removed to avoid blockages when the *churro* comes out of the machine. If you leave them and mix them back in, the *churros* will end up coming up deformed and you'd have to start again, removing the hard parts later.

The *churro* comes out of the machine in the form of a star, with a fairly small centre. When picking up a piece of dough to put into the machine, you need to knead it again with your hands covered in oil, which will make it smoother.

PREPARING "*CHURROS*"   267

The machine has a kind of hollow, steel cylinder through which the dough is fed. On one side, you put the dough in and out the other comes the *churro*. It works by using a rack and a piston which pushes below the dough, moved by a flywheel. One hand turns the wheel or pushes the pressure lever, while the other cuts off the *churros* with scissors. They fall directly into the hot oil, putting some oil onto the scissors every now and then so that the *churros* don't stick to them.

The length of each *churro* can be whatever you decide, but it's most common to be between ten and twelve centimetres. When you want to make longer ribbon or doughnut *churros*, one hand pushes out the dough, the other takes the *churros* out, and you can give them the shape you want when in the oil. This can be seen in the classic *churro* places in Madrid.

MIXER.   268

The basic principle is to cook the *churro* dough. There are electric mixers in which the tray for the dough is double which is also filled with oil and closed. Inside, it has electrical resistors which heat the body of the tray. When it is hot, you place the flour inside which is then worked and heated, If there are hard masses in the flour, you'll have to take it out and sieve it.

Of course, there are many ways that the flour can be heated: in an oven or in another container suspended over a sink of boiling water. In either case, it should be kept moving with the hands or a wooden spoon so that it doesn't form into thick clumps. To perfect it, you should pass it through a sieve. Once the flour is hot, you can put it into the machine. Mixing the boiling water with hot flour will cause the fusion to happen quickly at cooking temperature. If you are using an electrical machine without resistors, you'd have to heat the container from below so that the mixture stays as hot as possible.

ELECTRICAL MACHINES USED FOR MAKING *CHURROS*. 269

They are very similar to the manual ones except that the *churros* come out automatically. You cut them with a knife and put the pieces into the frying pan. They are regulated by the size of the *churro*. You can buy the machines in catering supply companies. If you want to buy them directly from a factory, check in the Yellow Pages in Valladolid (in Spain) in which there are various factories.

The oil used to fry *churros* can be used to fry other dough too, such as pies, pasties, croquettes and so on, as long as they don't leave behind their tastes. If the dough you fry is soaking wet with oil, because the oil was not hot enough, most of your customers won't come back. Accessories for *churro* machines. Among the accessories available are steel discs with different sizes for the *churros* to come out of, depending on how thick you want them.

You may have seen thick ones at fairs, filled with cream, which are made in the same way as the thin ones I described before. The disc is similar with but with a larger hole and a small metal piece in the middle so that it comes out hollow. In any case, the machine you buy will have various discs.

PRICES AND METHODS OF SELLING. 270

Churros may be sold at fairs in units or by the kilo. At restaurants, they are served in units and the calculations are done taking this into account. At fairs, they can be either in units or by the kilo. In street markets, they are usually sold by the kilo, with a sign saying so much money for a quarter or half a kilo. These prices need to be studied in advance to get more sales. There is one formula which never fails. When you want to sell a product, the first thing you have to do is to think as a customer. Set the price and conditions in the way that you would buy it being a customer. For example: if you offer iced drinks, a customer will want them big, cold, cheap and with a nice flavour. The salesman has to do everything to make their drinks like this and he will make good money. Psychology with customers is very important and something learned as you sell more and more.

CHURROS SOLD IN CORNER SHOPS AND ON THE MOVE. 271

There are mobile *churro* sellers at fairs and street markets around the country. Some are stalls which can be taken down, and others are installed into special vans. In both cases, the cooker, frying pan and work counter need to be available to make *churros*. Vans can be appropriately modified in specialised bodywork garages which are found in certain cities.

SELLING *CHURROS* AT FAIRS. 272

In fairs that last several days, *churro* sellers need to store all the prime materials they need, like flour, olive oil, gas, and other products. The taxes are usually moderate to low, though you then have to pay the appropriate municipality as well. If these fairs are in large cities or towns, the town hall will charge for the size of the location. In some cities, the best spots are sold at auction or they fix a price beforehand so that interested parties can get a good location. This is done quite some time in advance in the town halls in the largest municipalities.

FROZEN *CHURROS* FOR SELLING WHOLESALE. 273

The same churros that we made earlier are frozen and packaged.
Let me explain myself better. In terms of mass production, which is what we need to do, after mastering the preparation of the dough, we have to start thinking about how to make them quickly. As an idea, with an electric machine, we could be making *churros* and putting them on a baking tray with oil on it. They can have the form you choose. Then we can freeze them separately from each other so they don't stick together. We then put them in bags and keep them frozen for only about making money, things won't go so well. On hot sale. Later, I would look to doing the same with croquettes which we'll talk about later. We can offer them in shops or other businesses. You could also try pre-frying them lightly before freezing them. Through trial and error, you'll work out lots of things. When the customers buy them, they should let them thaw a little and then fry them in hot oil. In the packages or bags, you could have a note with the preparation method. Flour, water and salt along with some other possible ingredient without talking about exact amounts or percentages.

MANUFACTURING THICK, SOFT *CHURROS*. 274

This is made with flour at room temperature (not hot as before). Use a large bowl, as the mixture will grow in size due to the yeast. Half a litre of warm water, 25 grams of yeast which is used to make bread, (a pinch of salt, lemon juice mixed with water and two spoonfuls of olive oil). To this we add 700 grams of flour, mixing and working it to get rubbery dough. Keep working it until it is elastic and soft. This is left to stand until the size is almost double. When it has risen, we hit it a few times to get it back down and when it starts to rise again, start making the *churros*. Introducing the dough into the machine is done with a wooden spoon or pallet or similar, since the dough has to be soft and hard to manage with the hands. Some people use this machine I mentioned earlier.

Other traditional professionals use a manual machine in which the *churros* are forced out by turning a handle, holding the machine against the chest. Again, the dough when it comes out is placed into the hot oil immediately and is left to form a long spiral. Once the spiral is made, with the help of two wooden sticks, lift the centre of the spiral so that it doesn't burn and finish frying the outside which started being fried later. Then you need to turn over the entire spiral, and when it is done, take it out and drain the oil.

This can possibly also be done with the machine we mentioned at the start if we add 25 grams of oil to the water and another 100 grams of flour per litre of water before mixing in order to make it a bit drier and the *churro* easier to handle. I say possibly because it's a question of trying. If they don't come out correctly, trial and error will help you decide if the proportions are flexible. Not all types of flour have the same moisture content, so you'll have to try with different ones. They can be sold in units or by the kilo.

FRITTERS. 275

The recipe for this dough is the same as with the thick *churros* though they can be a little less soft. This dough is made with hands wet with water or oil so that it doesn't stick. When it starts rising, hit it a little to get it down, and when it starts to rise again, you can start making fritters, small doughnuts or flat cakes. They are sold either by units or by kilo, depending on the market they are in.

PREPARING FRITTERS. 276

We have the hot oil, the container with the dough and hands wet with water. With one hand, take a fistful of the dough and, squeezing it, make a ball whatever size we want between the index fingers and thumbs. With the other wet hand, we take the ball and put it in the frying pan. This is quick and we have a few in the pan, we roll them around using a skimmer until they are fried. Take them out, drain the oil out and they're done. They can be sold as they are, rolled in sugar or filled with cream like the ones you see in bakeries covered in sugar. You can fill them by half-cutting them with a knife or scissors, and then put cream in using a spoon or a squeezable tube. You should remember that the ones made in bakeries are made in a different way using eggs.

FRIED FLAT CAKES. 277

With this same dough, you can make flat cakes in the same way. You take a larger ball of this dough, and flatten it, turning it with the hands, in the same way they make pizzas to stretch them. When they are large and round, put them carefully in the hot oil. Be careful when you put it in: the oil burns. Then you just turn it over so that both sides are fried. When you take them out of the frying pan, put them vertically to drain the oil, standing them in a special stand. If you leave them horizontally stacked up, you won't get rid of the excess fat and you can't eat so much fat.

BERLINERS (ANOTHER TYPE OF DOUGHNUT). 278

Place inside a large pot which has space for the mixture to grow: 500 grams of water and
25 grams of yeast, 25 grams of oil, 50 grams of sugar, mix it all well, then add 800 grams of flour. Knead it all together until it becomes elastic, similar to dough for bread or buns. The proportions can be increased or decreased.
The dough should have the same feel as that of bread or buns - soft and manageable with the hands - so that they form balls and hold their shape without being hard. Take a portion of this dough without waiting for it to rise a second time. Make equal portions and, with a hand wet with oil, form balls on the counter. These balls are made by rolling them in a circle with the palm of the hand. Their size should be around that of a small orange or a tennis ball, since it will grow to almost twice the size. Put them on baking trays covered in oil with space between them, so that they don't stick together when they grow and deform (in this case, the dough is harder and keeps its shape). When they grow, they are ready to be fried.

Take them one by one, carefully so that they don't shrink again, and put them in a frying pan with hot oil. you have to keep moving them right away so that it has a uniform colour. When they are done, take them out, drain them and, still hot, roll them in sugar, put them on a tray, sprinkle cinnamon on them and they're done. The same price has to be less than any other bakery since we have to beat off any other competition. The price can be in units or by the kilo. All of these fried pastries can be served to the public in bags or special paper wrappers which absorb the oil, for the good of the customer and our future sales. In general, dough which doesn't have fat inside, like *churros* as I explained, have a limited life space, since only a few hours after starting, they become hard and lumpy. If it's a day with lots of rain, they become soft and lumpy.

CREAM FOR FILLING DOUGHNUTS AND SO ON. 279

Cream used in bakeries is very easy to make: it takes a litre of milk, grated lemon peel, three hundred grams of sugar, a hundred grams of flour and a few drops of egg-coloured food colouring. If you want the best quality, put four egg yolks in for every litre of milk.

Recipe: Put the milk on the cooker, and in a separate container, put sugar and flour, well-mixed together. If you put egg yolks in, put them in the container with the dry mixture (the one with flour and sugar mixed together). Next to this, dissolve the egg yolks with a little milk, then, one mixed, add a little more milk at room temperature, and dilute the egg, milk, sugar and flour until it is completely mixed and dissolved. When the mix starts to boil, add the contents of the sugar, flour and egg yolk the milk and keep stirring it until the mixture is uniform. Remember to stir right to the bottom of th container with the wooden spoon or whisk, so that it doesn't stick, and so that it cooks well throughout the mixture. After fifteen or twenty seconds of boiling, it is done. If you use egg yolks, they may give the colour needed so you won't need the colouring. If you don't have enough colour in spite of the eggs, you can always add a few drops of colouring. If you want to be sure the cream won't go sour, make it with half milk and half water. To be even surer, in summer, you can use only water.

CHOCOLATE-FLAVOURED CREAM. 280

If you keep some of the same cream from the previous paragraph, add some cocoa powder and mix it well, you have chocolate-flavoured cream. To make sure it comes out well, without lumps, mix 100 grams of cocoa powder with (a very little) lukewarm water and mix it with half of the cream we made earlier. If it isn't pure cocoa and it is pre-prepared hot chocolate, you'll need a bit more, since the proportion of cocoa in these powders is no more than 30% of the total.

VEGETABLE FOOD COLOURING. 281

To be clear: in the same way that there is egg-yellow food colouring, there is also strawberry, orange, vanilla, coffee, chocolate, mint, lemon and any other you want, and there are also essences of any flavour. In general, colouring is sold in powder and can be bought from bakery suppliers, as well as preservatives and others authorised by law. When I say a few drops of colouring, it's because bakeries have ready-made bottles with water to control the amount you put in. Fifty grams of egg-yellow colouring powder can be mixed with a litre of water, shake it and it's ready to use. You have to be very careful when putting in food colouring that the drops fall as actual drops and don't put it more than necessary. If you put it too much, the food will go back and you'll have to throw it out. Example of colouring and essences (I used to use them too to make ice lollies): An ice lolly, the type we liked when we were little, contain the following: to make a litre of liquid which will make 20 lollies, approximately, you need a litre of water, three tablets of saccharine dissolved in the water, four or five drops of essence (using a dropper) of the flavour you want, and a few drops of colouring. Strawberry ice lollies have: strawberry essence, strawberry colouring and the sweet saccharine. Strawberry ice-cream, for example, normally contains strawberries, but not enough to give in the correct colour and flavour, so you need to add colouring and essences. Of course, there are some Italian and Valencian artists who make ice-cream very well.

EXAMPLES OF COLOURING AND ESSENCES. 282

When I give an example, I'm trying to explain this reality which surrounds us. And you, as an entrepreneur, mustn't ignore any knowledge which might make you rich one day. Why do I specify saccharine here, and not sweeteners or sugars as it says in food packaging labels? Because I'm not sure if you understood me. If we make ice lollies with sugar instead of saccharine, when they come out of the freezer, they will be hard since they work at very low temperatures. When you have them ready for sale, the freezers will be at around 18 or 20 degrees below zero (approximately) and they will melt and become watery, which won't happen with saccharine. Tastes and colours dominate the food market. If food colouring and salt didn't exist, many businesses would be ruined. There are many people who think that you can't eat without salt. We are lucky we have so much salt in mines and in the sea.

SLICED POTATOES. 283

Since only a little while ago, the stands that sell *churros* in fairs and others... buy potatoes already cut and frozen, some very thin and others thicker, in the form of crisps. They either make them themselves or they buy them in individual bags, ready to sell. This means less work and a better final product than on-the-spot manufacture.
Crisps, sold in individual bags, which look like they contain more than they do, can be made like anything else. You can

make them with industrial or manual machines, then you put them in water for an hour and then fry them. Drain the water and fry with hot oil. Put them loosely in the frying pan so they don't stick together and keep moving them so they are fried evenly. Once the excess oil has been drained, put them in an airtight container or in packets as quickly as possible so that they stay crunchy. Humidity and airborne dust will ruin them. Old potatoes are better for making both crisps and potato wedges. If the crisps are open to the air for a long time without being in airtight containers, when you open the bag, they will be soft and not crunchy. Potato wedges. You need to peel them and cut them into segments. Put them a little while in water, drain and fry them. When you have a business in which you sell food as you fry it, it's common to half-fry a certain amount in reserve and, when you want to sell them, put them in hot oil and finish frying them quickly.

PRE-COOKED FROZEN POTATOES. 284

They are sold wholesale in bags of five or ten kilos, which are usually used in large catering firms. Supermarkets sell bags of one or two kilos for sale to customers. They are being used more because they are prepared so quickly. The industrial method of creating these frozen potatoes is: the pre-cooking needs to be finished as cheaply as possible. The most expensive raw material used is oil and you need to avoid using it up excessively. Business is business, and customers will be happy as long as the product is prepared and is good quality. Of course, we also have to consider competition, and profits are fundamental to any business we run. The main theme of this book is how to make money.

INDUSTRIAL PROCESS FOR FROZEN POTATOES. 285

You can try this in advance since the type of potato varies from region to region or country to country. Wash and peel by machine or hand. Cut them into wedges, again either by a machine which makes the individual cuts or by hand. Once you've washed and drained the wedges, boil them in water for two minutes or less in a normal pan (not a fast-cook one), and take them out carefully, making sure they don't break or stick to one another, so that they are all cooked at the same rate. Take them out of the water and drain them well. Then put them in hot oil uniformly, turn them over without them breaking, and take them out quickly. We don't want to fry them completely. Finally, drain the hot oil. We will have made them a bit softer so that cooking them later will be quicker and effective, and the surface fat will be looser. Then freeze them.

FREEZING EN MASSE. 286

You can freeze them in groups or separately if they are to be used in a pub. For mass production and selling wholesale, it's vital to have the right premises, the sanitary permit and so on. What seems more complicated is freezing the potatoes without them sticking together. Actually, this is a simple process. After taking them out of the frying pan and draining the oil, put them on a conveyor belt, separated in a row, which passes under a fan, so that the wedges cool down. On the same belt, they go straight to an ultra-fast freezer so that they are frozen and separate. At the end of this process, we put them in bags with our brand on it and other information, such as the weight, and then keep them frozen. Then they are sold to wholesalers, large warehouses, pubs, restaurants and hotels. You have to try this yourself first a few times to make sure they come out well.

WINE *PESTIÑOS*. 287

The recipe is as follows: a litre of white wine, half a litre of oil, a pinch of salt, some aniseed and flour. Heat the oil and when it's hot, throw in a slice of lemon or orange peel. Take it off the heat and wait for it to cool. Once the oil is cold, put it in the mixing bowl, and add the wine and aniseed. Then you will add flour until the dough is tough and manageable. The amount of flour depends on the humidity it contains. Add enough until the dough is hard and well-mixed. You make it by pressing with the fists each time you add flour until it disappears. You can also use a dough mixing machine if you have one, especially if you want to go into mass production for selling to wholesalers. The dough is hard but manageable due to the amount of fat it contains.

FORMING THE *PESTIÑOS*. 288

To form it as perfectly as possible, working manually, put some dough on the work counter, and with a rolling pin, roll it until it is about three or four millimetres thick. Then use a mould or glass, about five or six centimetres wide, to cut out equal slices. To get them ready to put in the frying pan, take a slice of the dough, wet your fingers with water, and fold it in half, pushing the two sides together to make them stick, forming a kind of tube or small "basket", and put them smoothly into the frying pan with hot oil, moving them to ensure they cook evenly. Once you take them out, let the oil drain out. If you work like in mass production, you can have a simple machine, formed by two rollers and a handle. One of the rollers will have the blades which will cut the dough into circles, ovals, squares or rectangles. The machine will allow you to make the dough either more or less thick. I ended up making this machine myself to make the process easier. If these parallel rollers are laminated, they will last forever. I don't invent anything. I adapt other people's ideas for my convenience. It's a reflection of what businesses will do. In food machine shops, you can see many tools which are easy to use, very interesting and easy to adapt to any other job, sometimes different from the ones they were made for. It's all a question of making our most loyal worker do something - <u>our brain</u>.

FINISHING OFF THE *PESTIÑOS*.   289

There are various ways to do it, one of which is that once the oil has been drained but they are still hot, put some sugar on them so they stick well as well as making them heavier. You have to know both the price per kilo and the price per unit, because customers will buy in both ways. If the *pestiños* are cold, boil some water and put the *pestiños* in a sieve or colander. Hold them up for a few seconds in the steam the water gives off, and then you can add sugar to them. Another way of adding this sugar bath: put water and sugar in a pan to boil, and when the sugar is a little thick (you'll know by putting the end of a fork in the sugar which is boiling) and when they stick to your fingers, take the liquid off the heat. Dip a wooden spatula in the melted sugar and rub it on the side of the pan.
You'll get a white layer on the surface of the liquid. Do it a few times, and you can dip them in and then take them out again as quickly as possible. Then you can leave them to drain in a wire sieve or on the work counter.
 Carry on doing this until you've done enough to fill the table or on wooden frames. If the sugar gets cold, heat it up with a splash of water until it boils a little, and use the same process. Every time you dip the *pestiños* in sugar using this method, you only serve them when they're totally dry. You can then

put them in dishes in various groups, as long as they aren't sticking together. For wholesale, they should be packed in separate units in either plastic bags or cellophane wrapping. You could also put onionskin paper or something else convenient on the inside of 500-gram cardboard boxes to avoid the humidity entering. The boxes would have the upper part of the cellophane open so that you can see the product. These 500-gram boxes can be sold in bulk wholesale, four or five kilos at a time. By doing this, no-one between the manufacturer and the customer will touch the product.

ANOTHER COATING FOR *PESTIÑOS*. 290

If we put sugar and water to boil, when it is sticky to the touch as I mentioned earlier, put a bunch of *pestiños* in a sieve or colander and hold it over the water to be heated by the steam. When they are really humid, put some icing sugar on top which we have ready on the table (icing sugar is normal sugar, ground up and made into powder) which can be bought from bakery supplier and wholesalers. Dust this sugar on and shake a little to remove any excess which didn't stick. Once you're finished, put them on a dish for shops or cafés, or wrap them up for wholesale. You can also try using castor sugar.

CLARIFICATION ON THE POINT OF USING SUGAR WHEN BOILING. 291

When we heat up sugar and water, as it boils, the water evaporates. To check the thickness of the boiling sugar, put the end of a fork, or similar, so that you can try touching the sugar with the fingers. The first thing to check is whether it is sticky, as we said before. This is when we have "weak threads". As the water boils more, if we touch and separate our thumb and index finger after dipping them in this boiling liquid, it will form a thread, and now we have "strong threads". Then when you take a little of that melted caramel in your fingers (the ones you tested the other sugar with) and you can make a little ball with your fingers, keep boiling the water and that ball will stretch out. Put it in water in a cup and split it in half, and you will see a crystal which will be the end of the caramel. Continue boiling it and it will become burnt caramel for flans and so on. Do this with a form and make sure your fingers are wet so you don't burn them.

PASTY DOUGH. 292

This dough I describe is very common and ideal for pasties. In a bowl, we put: 200 grams of margarine, 150 grams of sugar, four egg yolks, a whole egg and half a cup of aniseed. Mix these ingredients until you get a soft paste. Add 400 grams of flour and mix it in until uniform. Put the dough on the work counter and dust it with flour, so that it doesn't stick to the counter, the rolling pin or your hands. This can be used for any types of pasties, or as the basis for cream or fruit pies, etc. This should always be cooked in the oven.

SWEET PASTIES. 293

Roll out the dough with a rolling pan on the work counter until it is three or four millimetres thick. Cut out some circles with a mould around six or seven centimetres wide. Put a spoonful of jam or any other sweet substance in the middle. Then paint the edge of the circle you cut out with water, fold it to make a semi-circle with the jam in the centre. At the edge where the halves are joined, pinch them together with a fork or anything else similar to make them stick together. re is a specific bakery tool for this which is a kind of small serrated wheel with an axis and a handle, which you use to roll it out as if it were a spur. Roll it around the edge of the dough and it will stay together. These pasties are placed in a baking tin and left to cook. While they are still hot, pour on some icing sugar and they're ready. If you want better quality, make them with the dough used for *pestiños* and, after they are fried, fry them lightly in melted sugar while they are still hot. Or dampen them with water vapour from boiling sugar and dust them with normal icing sugar.

SAVOURY PASTIES. 294

You make them with puff pastry and you can make them a bit bigger, since they can be eaten for snacks instead of a sandwich. The mould to cut them could be a bigger circle or rectangle and can be painted on the outside with beaten eggs before putting them in the oven. You can put anything tasty you want inside them. You could use flakes of fried fish with tomato; cooked and salted fish with a sauce; ground meat, fried with a sauce; diced chicken with fried tomato; fried sausages, and so on. It's a good idea to do something to be able to tell them apart just by looking, either different sizes or styles. Some could be longer, others squarer, and you'll be able to tell the difference easily. A good cook will know how to do this much better. And if they don't, you can teach them with these explanations.

Savoury pasties usually sell very well if the quality and price are well-calculated. If you sell them wholesale, it's like any other industrial food product. You need to add the legal preservatives. I know of one person who, for a lot of time, worked on his own as a baker, selling to customers as well as wholesale. He then moved to another building to dedicate his business exclusively to wholesale. These days, his speciality is industrial bakery products, wrapped individually and biscuits in general. He sells throughout Spain and part of Europe. Every type of pasty can be sold finished, ready to eat, or uncooked and frozen for wholesale as frozen products.

INEXPENSIVE JAMS. 295

When I talk about being economical, I'm not talking about saving money. I refer to investing in small businesses and making more money. We've seen that some businesses, such as cafés, make natural orange juice and throw away the peel. Jam factories use the whole orange. To make jam, do the following: wash the entire oranges in machines or by hand, with a stiff brush to leave them completely clean, removing any impurities. The skin, after the juice has been sold in the café, can be taken advantage of by placing it for a day in water to soften and moisten. You then grind it up using a machine without making it too fine. It should end up as grains. Weigh the orange pulp and add the same amount of sugar with a little water to boil, making sure you watch it and stir it now and again to make sure it doesn't burn. The water will evaporate and the sugar becomes thicker. When it is thick and has a point, as we discussed earlier, you could say that it is done. Then you package it in bottles, making sure the lid is tight. Boil them in a double saucepan for 25 to 30 minutes and they're done. Store them in packages with the date and contents. Of course, for the jam to come out really fine, you need to put it in a blender.

Other fruits used for jams can be prepared by removing the skin and stones, dicing them or cutting into small piece and adding the appropriate sugar. For diced fruit, such as pears, apples, peaches and so on, peel them, remove the stones and imperfections, dice them up and put as much as you can into glass jars. Then add a soup spoon full of sugar and fill with water until almost full - leave about half a centimetre - close it well and boil in a double saucepan.

CABELL D'ÀNGEL ("ANGEL HAIR")   296

To make this Spanish delicacy, use pumpkins with skin mottled with greens and whites. They are only used for the hair and the slices of crystallised fruit. To make *cabell d'àngel*, cut the pumpkin into two or three slices, put it them the oven and cook them covered in aluminium foil so that they don't burn. Once they are cooked, using a spoon, you'll be able to take out the pulp very easily, leaving the skin totally bare, without flesh. Then take out the seeds. Take apart the pulp with the hands leaving it as densely-packed strands. Then you put it to boil, adding the same weight of sugar as *cabell d'àngel*, and a very little water to help it boil. Stir it now and again to make sure it doesn't burn. The flame should be strong until it boils, watching it closely, and then lowering the flame so it doesn't burn, until there is no water left. Then package it and boil it in a double saucepan as mentioned earlier.

CRYSTALLISED FRUITS. 297

For crystallised fruit, cut the pumpkin into medium-sized slices and remove the skin which is hard. Remove the seeds and cut the flesh into regular slices. Leave it in water for eight hours, remove and drain. Then, in a container, cover them with clean water and add 600 grams of sugar for every kilo of pumpkin. Put it to boil until cooked and the liquid becomes thick. Finally, keep them in a cool place for a while, covering the liquid and keeping it thick. The soft parts of the flesh which come loose from the slices can be used to make *cabell d'àngel*. To crystallise them (the coating of sugar on the outside), you do the same as with *pestiños* (by rubbing the sugary liquid on the sides of the pan). When you rub the sides with the wooden pallet, it produces a thick white sugar which sticks to the fruit when dipped inside. Every time you want to coat various fruit, keep rubbing the sides of the pan to make a whitish liquid which sticks to the fruit. Give it the sugar coating, take them out with a spoon and let them drain on mesh stands on the table. After a few hours, they'll be dry. Take the stands, supported from below by the hand so that the coating doesn't break and fall from the fruit. Wrap them in boxes with the bottom and sides made of waterproof paper or in cellophane so that they don't stick and lose their coating. If they don't become solid, it's because the boiling and thickness of the sugar were not enough. You could also wrap them in groups and sell by the kilo or other moderate size.

FRUIT COATED IN CHOCOLATE. 298

This is done with chocolate melted using a double saucepan. Put the coating in a container over another which contains hot water which will melt the coating without boiling it. The slices of fruit, drained in advance, will be put one by one in the chocolate and taken out quickly, leaving them to dry. This can be done with a fork, one after another. Take it out of the chocolate and place it on a rack to drain or on the work counter, separated until they dry. If there are any lumps or flecks of chocolate, cut them off with scissors. Wrap them with onionskin paper or cellophane. The portions are usually similar in size to scones, more or less. You may have a machine to do this job. You'd need to look in bakery machine shops.

You can also do them in small slices, like smaller chocolates after the chocolate coating is dry, wrap them like a sweet and sell them as fruit chocolates with the name you want to give them. Example: "Paris Fruit Chocolates", or whatever is the name of your town or city. You can do them of any type of fruit, like cherries in syrup, peach slices, plum, etc.

In bakery suppliers, they sell boiled fruit in syrup in tins of up to five kilos. They have been treated, as we've discussed, peeled, cleaned and boiled with water and sugar. Be careful they don't break or fall apart when you pick them up. Fruit which is slightly green but not yet fully mature can also be used for this though not jam. Do the same process, boil the fruit with a good, thick sugar, drain and dry them, and then coat with chocolate. And here we have another product for wholesale. (Fruit, both tinned or natural, has to be boiled and drained enough before any crystallising or chocolate coating is applied.)

Chocolate used for this can be bought from bakery suppliers and is used as it comes. You don't need to add anything. If you want, you can try adding a few grams of butter. Chocolate which is left over can be left in the pan or you can put it on the counter so that, after it dries, you can keep it for when you use it again. This chapter, as well as being good for cafés and restaurants is also useful for wholesale.

CHAPTER 8   299

CAFÉS SELLING HOT CHOCOLATE, *CHURROS*, GRILLED CHICKEN, LEMONADE AND SO ON. 300

A café which specialised in hot chocolate and *churros* is another idea. I'm going to explain how to make a good business, not just another one in the market. Throughout this book, I insist that the fundamental thing is to find the ideal place to set up any business. In this case, you need to consider the public this specialist café is aimed at.

Ideal places for these businesses. At the beginning, I'd say that you see *churro* stalls at fairs, in weekly street markets in towns and cities, in some pedestrian streets in any city or district, and in busy tourist areas. Around some permanent markets in cities, etc. You can also put them in other unexpected places like with any business. The customers that come into this type of business are the working class, who are the majority.
 Essentials to sell plenty during the whole day. In order to be a good business, we should design it like any other pub or café. The tax on these businesses is the lowest in the catering trade. Work can start in the morning with breakfasts of all types (and, of course, hot chocolate and *churros*), then continue with lunches, sandwiches and so on. In the afternoon, back to *churros* at specific times for the customers who come to buy them to take out or for an afternoon snack. This business, as long as they are well-run with the formula we discussed before, can work very well if the midday gap is covered with other food. And since we are trying to make it popular, we'll keep going with what comes next.

GRILLED CHICKEN. 301

At midday, customers don't want hot chocolate. They want normal food or meals at a good price. Having a wall-mounted chicken rotisserie - which sells more - may be useful for attracting more customers (and better publicity for increasing sales of grilled chicken, either to eat in or take away). This business would be quite complete and would help fill out the cycle of sales at the best times of the day. Anything can be sold at any time but some times are good for certain things and some sell more than others.

Hot chocolate with *churros* and breakfasts in general begin in the morning and you can add sandwiches and iced drinks in summer, which can be sold all day. When lunchtime draws closer, this is followed by grilled chicken and other fried food, to eat in or take away. You can have offers like in any popular menu. Also well-accepted are set meals with quarter or half a chicken with chips, served to tables with drinks and other accompaniments.

When the customers read: "Portion of chicken with chips, croquettes and tomato, so much money", this is tempting for many people. At a good price, many customers will come in without a doubt. Then we also have the menu in which the meals offered are listed as well as chickens to take away. This service can be served in various sizes are good prices. For chickens to take away, chips, croquettes and so on have their own separate prices. Then you also have drinks and bread, also charged apart but at a good price, so that customers come back. If you want to make money on sides because you don't get much on the food, the customers need to know the prices.

Customers won't come back if the prices are too high. If you sell at a good price which makes you a profit, sales will keep increasing. You can also set a simple meal with a drink and bread. Ah! And if you can get your customers used to eating in the street, with a paper cone of your chips or croquettes, your business will be popular pretty quickly. Customers are always waiting for competitive entrepreneurs with new and original business ideas. Customers are the best treasure that a businessman can have. If we don't let them down, they won't let us down. On the other hand, if a chicken has a certain price to be taken out, the price for eating in can be higher - without being ridiculous - to pay for the service.

Instead of thinking about selling ten or fifteen chickens making 40% profit on each one, be happy with fewer profits and selling a lot more, and your sales will go up. These chicken meals can be accompanied by chips, two lettuce leaves, two slices of tomato, and two croquettes, placed on a large dish or plate. If the prices are set to sell a lot, your business will work from day one. You can also offer plates of croquettes or chips made on the spot with prices we have worked out in advance.

SELL WHAT WE MAKE OURSELVES. 302

When we offer competitive prices and impeccable service, customers will come in more or less continuously. If meals are served to tables in plastic cartons, we are making the food look worse. The same food to be taken out can be in plastic, but to eat in, we'll give our food better quality if we serve it on normal plates and with normal cutlery. As you can see, even if you have to spend a little more on plates and so on, our sales will go up to compensate (although we still need plastic packages for take-away food).

What am I trying to say with these comparisons? The businesses you set up, or the ones I'm talking about here, are not new and many other competitorS will have the same ones. Yours have to be different in some way, working intelligently, offering quality at a good price. In this way, you'll be competitive and keep selling in spite of the others.

Even if they still haven't, they'll soon copy your ideas. Don't forget however that the first one to come up with an idea has a head-start by getting the best customers, which you then have to know how to keep.

SETTING UP THE BUSINESS AND HOW IT WORKS. 303

You need a place with many pedestrians as I mentioned earlier, made up of a sales counter, made of any material, and with a stainless steel top, and the space and tables for customers. It can easily work like many other similar businesses in which the customer orders at counter, either for take-away or to eat in. If they want to eat in, charge them in advance and take the food to their table on trays on plates. You can have self-service with breakfasts, hot chocolates, *churros* and sandwiches. At midday and meal times, as well as what we've already mentioned, you can sell various types of omelettes, fried food (chips, croquettes, pasties) and other suitable food which is easy to make. Some things may be better served by a waiter or waitress and so shouldn't be available as self-service. When we set up this type of business, which may include a café, we have to be aware that we'll have many competitors of the same type. The customers prefer the business to be acceptable, clean, have good customer service, and all at a good price. Prices in a café can't be as low as this type of popular business. The prices have to be based on charging below those of the competition. Every product sold has to be made like a speciality, charging acceptable profits so that customers keep coming back, regardless of the competitors. If the prices we put are the same as in any other business, we won't get provide anything original and customers won't travel long distances.

PACKAGING FOR TAKE-AWAY FOOD. 304

You need various types of these, including cups, for all types of take-away food and drinks, including chickens and hot chocolate. There are various types and styles which are already suitable for certain services. There are ones with lids for chicken, chips, croquettes and other hot food, as well as paper sachets which work as a kind of cone. Sandwiches to be taken out can be wrapped in napkins and put in paper or plastic bags. As a general package for transporting various products, plastic bags with handles are essential for customers to carry their food comfortably. This is all part of good customer service. You can also use cups for iced drinks, for serving inside or taking out with a lid.

OTHER USEFUL ITEMS FOR THE DINING ROOM. 305

Not many businesses serve food to tables with plastic, as if the food was second-class, making sure the money that comes into the till is legal currency. This is something psychological, but is serving food in plastic a good idea? No, the customers want good food at good prices, but if we reduce its class by serving it in plastic, it loses some of its appeal. In my opinion, after having worked in the +world of both small and medium-sized businesses, which is what I'm teaching you, I think that food is served best on good quality plates with stainless steel cutlery. They may be more work to collect and wash, but, dear reader, when you think about any business, you have to put yourself in the customer's shoes and not think about profits.
They only come if you use suitable equipment. Imagine that you go to a pub and order half a chicken with chips, or a sandwich and a drink. If the plates and glasses are plastic,

while in other places they give you the same food at the same price on normal plates, you'd go to the one with better service. If you're competitive in service and price, you'll sell more. Your business will sell and sell. What you feel is best for you as a customer is what you should offer your customers. Applying this formula to your plates, your business may become a good restaurant and, with time, something even greater. The real reason customers come back is if they go away happy, and this will make a normal business into a good one. When customers become regulars, that's when you start on the road to riches.

Setting up the premises. The measurements of the building you use may be seventy, eighty, a hundred square metres or even more. It all depends on your luck with finding a good location. Horrible, deteriorated premises in a good commercial location in the right area is more positive and profitable than premises which look lovely but have everything in a place with no pedestrians. The kitchen could have a partition counter which could be made of glass brick. Customers like to see something, even if it's only the chef's white hat. With the glass brick wall about a metre twenty in height, they can see enough but not too much. The chicken rotisserie and *churro* machine can be in view and seen to be working, even if they aren't too close. It's all good publicity.

EXTRACTOR FAN IN THE KITCHEN. 306

This is something essential, by law, since your customers mustn't be breathing smoke from the kitchen, even if the kitchen door is kept closed. If it is strong enough, as well as removing smoke from the kitchen, it will also renew the air in the public area. It's a good idea and no-one will complain about the air they are breathing.

TAKE-AWAY COUNTER. 307

This should be situated near the door of the business along with the take-away food with enough space for people to buy and sell comfortably. It will have various display windows with the products available (*churros*, chickens, and so on). They can be placed on trays in mentioned in previous chapters. The counter can be elongated and adapted for the kind of service in pubs where the customer can also take the food to the tables themselves. In general, *churros* are served freshly made as we've already seen. They become hard over time because they are made with dough without fat.

TABLES FOR EATING IN. 308

If we set up the business for both eating in and taking away, we need to offer services like in pubs. One area for serving to the public and another for eating in, where the tables and seats for customers are. Rather than wasting time washing tablecloths, some people cover the tables with a tablecloth and then put glass which doesn't break easily on top of that. This also looks good. You could also put individual paper coasters down. Likewise, paper napkins can be put on each table.
The premises must have the appropriate public toilets, a small warehouse, an administration office, etc., as explained in previous chapters. Don'tforget that the kitchen needs to have good ventilation for smoke and a connection to the bar or counter. The layout can be different in each premises, but I would remind you that the kitchen doesn't necessarily need to be in a separate room, enclosed by walls.

CLASS OF RESTAURANT. 309

The classes of popular café, pub or restaurant are about the same. They are classed as working class ("popular") pubs or restaurants which is enough to sell everything we've talked about. Despite everything I write here, the agency which knows the laws and which does the paperwork for you to open the business will have the last word. This type of business has to have various facets in order to be very profitable. I'm not going to talk about the question of sandwiches, portions of food and so on in this chapter, since I give plenty of explanations in others (look at take-away food, pubs and cafés, or in sandwiches). If you've read up to now, take your time and keep reading and you'll take in what you read. Keep improving your knowledge and, if you're motivated and determined, you'll be successful in everything you want to do.

MANAGING A BUSINESS IS AN ART WHICH IS LEARNED. 310

Customers adapt easily to directly buying their food. If not, you've got those hundred-year-old colas which always remind your customers that they need to drink and drink it. If our business sells hot chocolate and *churros* in the morning and afternoon, we need to plan to way to advertise, to let the public who might be interested in our business and come to visit us, as far away as they may be, and that we're waiting for them with *churros* and hot chocolate whenever they want them.
They'll end up getting used to consuming our products in this way. We'll advertise in the same way with our chickens, including putting the prices on view. I remember a fried fish business in Malaga. A small premises, a front counter made of white marble, leaning towards the customers' side and

trays or plates of all sorts of fried fish. Scales and a till. Of course, inside, they had their deep fat dryer and so on. The customers bought just as much to take away and eat on the street.

It's good to sell chips in paper sachets so the fat sticks to it. They sell very well and people like eating in the streets and, if not, they'll learn to. Future customers want to see an affordable price and that they don't feel confused because the place isn't presentable or too luxurious. If we want to make a lot of sales, we need to be prudent in order to see our income grow. There'll always be buyers with lots of cheaper sales and not with higher prices. Lots of cheaper sales will bring even more sales. If you don't know how to make hot chocolate, don't worry, keep reading, and I'll explain shortly how to make almost everything sold in this business. It's the only way to be competitive and profitable doing these activities. You can't underestimate your customers' intelligence. You can't cheat the customers. They need good service, quality and a good price. They are experts at buying and if they see something they don't like, they won't come back.

Customers are always willing to spend money unconsciously if you let them try your products for free. Sometimes, a free sample given to a customer can be enough for more people to buy your products. They'll get to know the product much earlier in this way and may buy more at your price. That's where large-scale publicity done by big businesses come from, and in a small business, why shouldn't we do the same

ADVERTISING. 311

When opening a business, selling products at almost cost price for a few days, even if you don't make any profits, can get you a lot of customers. You can also hand out discount vouchers in areas which are appropriate, indicating that they are valid for a particular day so that many customers don't go in on the same day to buy products with vouchers. They could be vouchers for 10 or 20% for whatever they buy. This publicity can be done during the first week or a little more. It's a way of advertising which you can reinvent yourself.

Of course, this is one idea for selling, but in one of our first businesses, selling iced drinks, the publicity was price, quality and coldness. The quality of the product was the taste, very sweet and cold with flakes of ice in the liquid. At about 23 or 24 years old, we set up a business selling *churros*, hot chocolate and ice-cream. Opening times, from 5 in the morning until 11 at night and selling all day long.

Publicity always gives good results if it's well directed. A week of working for less money doesn't matter if sales in the future are so much higher. That's the theory of the conquistador who isn't happy to taking over the castle but wants to have the whole kingdom.

These words might sound strange to someone who's never worked in business before, but for an entrepreneur it has to be part of their Bible, and finding a good suitable spot for the business is basic. Do you want more publicity? Do you want to sell *churros* in the afternoon? Hire a beautiful young lady to stand next to the front door, in high-heels and a miniskirt if you like, and with a tray of fresh sugary *churros* to offer to people passing in the street, served with tongs for hygiene's sake to avoid they take more than one. They might also have a look in the premises when they pass. The *churros* should be hot and fresh, the staff behind the counter should be dressed impeccably in white and ready to serve with good illumination. More than one of the tasters will go in to buy something. They'll see the business and read the price lists. It's important that the public know what each of the products you sell costs.

IMITATING ANTS. 312

We work with humans but watch ants when they walk around and they always go to the same place, right? Well no, sir, because if you put something near to their path, a few metres away, some grain or food which they can detect, they'll change their course. Customers will go into any premises where they are treated well and, if interested by the prices and service, they'll go out of their way to come to your business. But don't be complacent. A group of ants don't go somewhere for no reason. People do the same. If we let people know that there is something worth going out of their way for, a modern business with irresistible prices, we'll get them, but it's much better to have a better location which will get people in continuously.

SIGNS WHICH SELL. 313

A4-sized, white paper signs, written horizontally are easier to read. You can do it with a felt-tip pen if you're good at writing signs. You can put them on the inside of the premises and another one outside the door for people to see.
You can also do them on PC (if you don't have one, you can get a student to do them and get make photocopies of them and save them when the old ones are damaged, since good appearance is important). You have to make signs with only two or three lines which take up the who sheet and put them a visible position. You can also get a fast printer's shop to do it in large, clear, black letters for easy reading. The signs can say: "Grilled chicken to take away, x euros"; "½ chicken with chips, x euros"; "hot chocolate with *churros*, x euros". These signs are ideas which you can make better so that the image stays fixed in the retina of those who see it.
Customers want to see signs which say that you're almost

giving them food for free and you have to make their dreams come true. You have to adapt to the area and environment that surrounds you, modifying and improving your products and prices to sell a lot and make money. Businessmen are competitive, helpful and attentive, but they're not charities. Take into account that a picture sells more than a thousand words. People eat more with their eyes than with explanations.

ABOUT HOT CHOCOLATE. 314

The majority of customers in pubs or cafés want espresso. There are a small percentage who prefer whiter coffee which is easily resolved with a little more hot milk when serving them. If you ask for hot chocolate in a café, they serve you the milk and give you a packet of cocoa powder. You're not happy about it but you put up with it if they don't make hot chocolate themselves. For your business, you can buy bags of chocolate to make instant espresso. It will be more expensive for you than if you make it yourself and you won't be very competitive. You can also have it hot and ready to serve in a Thermos. In the chapter about cafés, I speak about flasks when sales are continuous. You really need to have two groups of instant coffee makers or four normal ones.

MAKE YOUR OWN CHOCOLATE. 315

Powdered chocolate in bags of five or ten kilos can be bought in food wholesalers who can supply many other products too. This type of powder is very common. Every manufacturer makes it in a different way (in terms of percentages of sugar, cocoa and flour). I'll explain to you later how to get it very good and cheap. Common chocolate powder has very little cocoa which is the most expensive ingredient. Test for making it as you like it. With the powder you buy (there are cheap powders which are not bad), you can try more things that I can explain to you. With that bag of chocolate you bought, half-fill a breakfast mug with fresh milk. Add a soup spoon of that powder and dissolve it very well so that there are no lumps when it boils. Put that mixture into a porcelain or steel jug, and put that to boil in the coffee machine (firstly removing all water vapour which remains inside, because it may come out very clear and not allow to you control the thickness. Cover the jug with a paper towel and hold it with the hand so that the chocolate doesn't come out while boiling. Once it is boiled, close the water inlet, and take out and clean the vaporiser with the paper napkin mentioned so that the chocolate doesn't dry out. Pour the chocolate into a cup and try it. With this test, you'll have worked out and controlled its thickness. If it isn't thick and sweet enough, you'll have to improve it yourself as I will explain to you next.

DEFINITIVE TESTS WITH THE CHOCOLATE. 316

Check the thickness and sweetness of the chocolate. If it isn't thick enough, add another half a teaspoonful of powder and try it again. it isn't sweet enough, add a little sugar and mix it well to avoid clumps of sugar when boiling. We've increased the quantity now. This mixture when dry should be mixed very well so that the hot chocolate comes out well. After a new mixture has been made, boil it like the other and pour into another cup. With this further test, you can check the sweetness and thickness and see if you are happy with it now. After two or three tests, you'll find the correct formula. This method using the coffee machine is fine if you don't sell much hot chocolate. Or you can start a new business in which you want to sell mainly chocolate. You could call is chocolate espresso.
If you sell a lot of breakfasts, a flask for the chocolate is vital.

Through these tests, you can work out the cost of a hot chocolate and sell at a good, competitive price, earning good profits. After the test, a mixture with a little more sugar, maybe a little flour (better if it is wheat starch) and the five- or ten-kilo bag of chocolate you bought. Once the dry mixture is made, put it in a sieve to make sure it is good quality; a bad-quality dry mixture of any product can spoil everything. Once the chocolate mixture is done, test it again with the coffee machine to see if it lacks either sweetness or thickness again and then modify it again. If it comes out very light - which may happen if there isn't enough cocoa - add a pinch of legal chocolate colouring. Be very careful! With the colouring, for a mixture with the entire ten-kilo bag, you should put in about "three fingers' worth". A good competitive price could be around 10% below the cost of your competitors and the mug served be bigger so that your competitors have two problems. Truly good-quality chocolate for selling wholesale is done by buying pure cocoa and the other ingredients, as I explain later.

HAVING HOT CHOCOLATE IN A FLASK READY TO SERVE. 317

You have to prepare it in a large pot or pan, knowing the proportions of each ingredient which you'll have written down in your little book. We make this chocolate in the same way as baking cream. Put 50% milk and 50% water into the pan we'll use for boiling. In another separate container, put in the chocolate powder according to the proportional calculations earlier (you can calculate this easily with scales or counting how many half-cups make a litre, and the same with the cocoa).

When the milk which is being boiled is still just warm, take lumps are left. When the milk starts to boil, pour the chocolate mixture into the milk and keep stirring it so it doesn't burn at the bottom, until it is completely boiled. Thirty or forty seconds more of boiling without stopping stirring it from the bottom and it will be ready, and you will have lost the flavour of the flour. Then you take it off the flame and put it in a flask. If it is too thick when you put it in the flask, add a little water to thin it out. If there is still some left at the end of the day, keep it in the fridge when it is cold. When you do this, make sure it is the first you sell the next day. If it's too thick, again, thin it down with drinking water. Never add more milk because you run the risk of it turning sour. When you make the chocolate, don't worry if it ends up thick – I'll explain that soon. What isn't good is if it ends up light. If you don't have a Thermos, and the chocolate is ready, you can heat it in the coffee machine when serving to customers. There are thickeners which used in catering. You can use wheat starch or corn starch when working out the recipe for hot chocolate and so on.

CRUNCHY, RECENTLY-MADE *CHURROS*. 318

Customers prefer them to be crunchy and recently-made. They like to see them being made which is why if the machine is on view, you sell more. Now I'll explain how you can make them and freeze them for wholesale, along with other products for your business. When fresh *churros* are sold, they are served in paper bags which, in turn, absorbs the oil. You also add some sugar on top once they are in the bag. *Churros* can be sold by the unit for breakfast or for taking away, or by the kilo.

 The sign could be something like: Churros, 500 gr., x euros, or similar. Always have your prices where customers can see them and the same price for all. In fair, they are sold in units at a dozen for so much money. They put a dozen, or whatever was ordered, into a triangular paper bag, like a cone, with tongs, a little sugar on top, give them to the customer and charge them. Four or five should be enough for breakfasts with hot chocolate and *churros*. You can also have pastries, French toast and other specialities of the house. Since *churros* don't have any fat (they are made only with water and flour), they don't stay tasty for very long. After a little time, they become dry and hard in summer, or soft and chewy in winter. This is why they are usually made as they are sold. When we talk about serving *churros* separately in the morning and afternoon, it's because you have to make them as you sell them at certain times, which the customers need to know in advance.

MORE ABOUT GRILLED CHICKENS.   319

More about these. Grilled chickens are sold in all cities and even more in busy areas. You can buy them clean and frozen, in various sizes and weights which is more practical. They are ready to be put on the rotisserie. You buy them in boxes of ten or twelve, weighing between a kilo and a kilo and a half. You can keep plenty of chickens in a chest freezer so that you never run out.Ideal chicken rotisseries. Vertical, wall-mounted chicken rotisseries are on view while they cook. They are a good source of publicity. Closed grills, like industrial electric ovens cook more quickly because they lose less heat. Customers understand what we're selling if they see the chickens going around through a window. There are butane and electric grills. In closed oven, the best thing is for them to have glass fronts which can be seen from the counter. You can buy a grill after seeing a few different ones working in other places which suppliers will have to sell.

ABOUT SELLING A LOT OF TOAST. 320

When you think about toast, it might seem like we're talking about tin loaves. The problems is that it is so expensive that, you can't be competitive with this in this type of business. To sell cheaper toast in cafés and so on, we use another type of bread. The baker can be in charge of this, by using loaves of bread, cut into slices by machines. If they cut them by hand, they can be cut diagonally so they are bigger and as thick as tin loaves of bread which might be a centimetre thick. Nobody has tried selling toast which is wrapped and frozen, ready to be heated. There can always be a first time. This is the advantage of having our brain working. It can always think about creating new, different products.

FRENCH TOAST WITH MILK. 321

They can be made with bread from the previous day which was left over and frozen. While frozen, we can still use them. If they are buns, remove a bit of the "belly" from the top, scrape away all hard parts, cut off the corners and make two halves from each one. If they are long loaves of bread, use a knife to scrape off any toasted or hard part and cut off the corners. Then you can cut it into slices as we've seen, to make them bigger. You can make the French toast as thick as you want, but it has to be equal. When you put milk on the slices of bread, make sure they aren't soaking wet and leave them on a tray. When the oil is hot, put beaten eggs onto the bread and fry it immediately. Put a few in a frying pan, turn them over so both sides become golden, and they're done. Here, we don't want to fry the bread. We want to fry the egg around it, so it's a question of almost throwing them in and taking them out. Finally, put them to drain without stacking them, so they don't break or get oil on each other. Then, when they are still hot, add a little sugar on both sides, put them in one layer on a tray, then add a little cinnamon and take them to the counter. If this is self-service, put them on individual plates for the customer to take. They can be heated in the microwave if they have waiting for a while.

FRENCH TOAST WITH WINE. 322

Dampen the bread with red wine, then beaten eggs and straight into the frying pan. When they are well drained, put on a little sugar and a small sign to keep them separate from the milk ones. You'll make the ones you need each day and they'll be good and tasty for the first three or four hours. After this time, you'll need to reheat them in the microwave before serving. They'll last a good few hours in a display window, and those left over at the end of the day shouldn't be served again (as I mentioned in the previous chapter on toast). The first entrepreneur who freezes French toast for wholesale will have an advantage. Then other businesses in the trade will copy.

SECOND BUSINESS: COPY THE FIRST ONE. 323

When a business is going well, the best thing is to repeat it in another area. You might say, "How can I? I can't multiply myself!" These businesses might be small but profitable. If you have to do everything, you'll never make enough money. Your first business should always be your take-off plan. You will choose one of your employees who has helped you so far to be in charge of your first business, it will continue working as you plan. You set up your second business and you run that with some help. You'll have enough time to be in both places when necessary and you'll be in charge of buying stock so you don't run out of anything in either place. This business will have a good chance of growing. Don't forget that when you need other employees is when you start making money. Remember: one person alone doesn't have time and can't ever be sick, and that businesses with other staff are the ones that will help you grow

CHAPTER 9   324

DIFFERENT PRODUCTS FOR SELLING WHOLESALE OR DIRECTLY TO CUSTOMERS.

HOT HOCOLATE POWDER.   325

The basic raw materials needed for hot chocolate sold in businesses are: cocoa powder, sugar, flour or wheat starch (the ones with fine powder similar to talcum powder made with flour or corn), some colouring and legal preservatives, vanilla, cinnamon and other scents. Every manufacturer has their own recipe and none of them have less than 25% cocoa in order to be acceptable. 30% cocoa should be enough to make good hot chocolate powder. It may happen that due to a lack of cocoa, you'll have a lack of colour, even though the taste is good. There are different types of artificial food colouring and one of them will be for hot chocolate powder. Three fingers' worth of colouring is enough for ten kilos of hot chocolate powder, a tiny amount. The proportion of additives may be written on the adjoining labels. All additives in powder will have been mixed up and will make a perfect mixture with the rest of the recipe.

HOT CHOCOLATE POWDER FOR SELLING 371 WHOLESALE.   326

The basics for making good and fine hot chocolate powder are: Get a mixing bowl and put in 35% pure cocoa; 35% flour starch (fine, like talcum powder) which can be bought in Riera Marsá in Barcelona or any other bakery supplier; and 30% ground sugar (icing sugar) which bakery suppliers, again, should have in stock; and a pinch of cinnamon powder and some kind of preservative. Mix it all together well and pass it through a fine sieve. Test it, as we've seen before. This mixture can be wrapped in individual bags to make one cup in a coffee machine. For selling wholesale, they should be put in boxes of around fifty units. They can also be sold in bags of 5 or 10 kilos to cafés or pubs, and smaller bags of 200 or 400 grams or whatever you like for selling to homes.

Check out similar products available in shops. You can also make hot chocolate which must be made with milk and will only contain cocoa, sugar, cinnamon and a preservative. You can try with 100 grams of icing sugar, 100 grams of pure cocoa and 10 grams of wheat starch or cornflour as we've talked about in powder. Mix it all well and sieve it well. Get a breakfast mug, fill it almost to the top with hot milk and two soup spoonfuls of the mixture, mix it with a spoon and it's ready to drink. Test it to make sure it's not too thick to drink. If there is not enough sugar or cocoa, add some.

Once you perfect it, you have another product to package for wholesale or in individual envelopes for making a single cup, and also to hotels as I said before. You can also try it without flour. If you put it in to be drunk, the cornflour or flour should be toasted. Otherwise, when being boiled, the flour inside is raw and doesn't come out well. Flour can be toasted in the oven or put in a pan on a flame but then you shouldn't stop stirring it until it is toasted. To be clear: For drinking chocolate, toasted flour or starch. For chocolate to be prepared, either boiled like instant chocolate, the flour or starch isn't toasted because it has to be boiled when being made.

MARKETING INSTANT HOT CHOCOLATE FOR PUBS AND CAFÉS. 327

Get an A4 sheet of paper, fold it twice vertically into a leaflet of three sheets, as if to put it in an envelope. Then, fold it in half horizontally and this will be approximately the size of an individual portion of instant chocolate. If it is drinking chocolate, the same size but with a different explanation. I've given you an idea about the same of a hot chocolate envelope so you know what I'm talking about. Then, you can hire a specialised printing shop to print out your designs on moisture-proof paper of around 7.5 x 9.5 cm in size or whatever measurement you feel is suitable for chocolate powder for a single cup. After you put the chocolate inside, you can close it using a cheap machine which seals the envelope and which can be found in any large machine shop, and there we have instant chocolate. The amount of chocolate you put in the envelope will have been decided by the tests you ran earlier. The envelope will be printed with your brand, an explanation of the product and its aim, and the contents with approximate percentages....,. Example contents: refined sugar, cocoa, starches, preservative and essences. Look at chocolate products sold in shops and you'll see what I'm talking about. These products are authorized by the Industry which a specialist agency could help you with.

If you don't have a coffee machine to do the test and you're not in the catering industry yet but you want to make instant hot chocolate, the best thing is to buy a home coffee machine and do the tests using that. In a breakfast mug, the type served in cafés, put half a cup of fresh milk and add two soup spoonfuls of the mixture we've made. Dissolve it and mix it with a teaspoon. Once the chocolate and milk are dissolved well, boil them in the coffee machine as we've see without any steam inside. But we're not finished here if we want to be sure. If the first test comes out very thick or very light, add or reduce the amount of chocolate. This is the only way you'll know the right amount of powder to use which you can weigh using scales. This quantity you weigh will be the amount that each individual envelope holds. If you don't have scales, you can measure the powder using a cup. You can prepare small boxes with your brand, each of which can hold fifty units to be used in pubs and so on. Once you know how to prepare the mixture, you can make various qualities to compete in the national market. The additives you might need for any product can be found in catering suppliers and they'll give you any extra information you might need. Any version of the recipe you make will have the same basic formula: the more cocoa, the lower the quality; the more flour, the thicker the result, and the lower the quality, etc.

As a thickener, I used flour (to be clear) and, at one time, agar, a thickening product. Flour or cornflour ground down to the thickness of talcum powder is a good thickener. Good suppliers can be found in Murcia, Spain to buy cocoa, cinnamon and other general spices. I used to buy the wheat starch we talked about in Riera Marsá. Powdered sugar (icing sugar), baking soda, margarine and everything you need that we've talked about can be found in the usual bakery suppliers. Everything you make can be used in your own business or for selling wholesale. To find suppliers in other areas, check the Yellow Pages for that area and you'll find telephone numbers for businesses in that city or area. This is how to buy directly from the manufacturer.

MANUFACTURE OF CROQUETTES. 328

As I explained, these croquettes can be sold in pubs, cafés, take-away food businesses or sold wholesale. The most important thing is mass production. You'll have seen different packaged, frozen food in supermarkets. Many croquettes are made with different fillings. The recipe and method of preparation are pretty easy. Some people have ideas for products or businesses and never make any money with them. Sometimes, others can bring them to fruition managed to give them the magic touch. Croquettes have existed for lots of years but if we bring our unique ideas about presentation and marketing, they can be the same as others but with a certain difference. To make the dough, follow the same recipe as with thin *churros*, bring water to the boil, heat the flour and mix them quickly. For croquettes, instead of water like with *churros*, use milk. The proportion is one kilo of flour to a litre and a half of milk.

METHOD OF PREPARATION FOR CROQUETTES. 329

Put some cold, well-diced onion in a pan on a low flame with 25 grams of margarine for every litre of milk (and a pinch of salt). If you make them with chicken, meat or any other raw product, it must be cooked or fried before being added. In this case, dice them very finely and sauté or fry them with the onion. You can also make them with fish, like cod, with the same process. Always make sure you remove all skin and bones, because in a croquette you can't have any type of hard materials. You could also put grilled chicken from the previous day which didn't sell which is diced well. You can also make them with ham and cheese. Wit 20 grams of cheese and 20 grams of sandwich ham well-diced for every litre of milk. The ham and cheese shouldn't be fried. Put them in milk before covering them in flour so that these slices are in croquettes. If you use chicken, meat or fish, about 40 grams of filling is enough for a litre of milk. Make sure that fish is sold without bones.

We should have the hot flour waiting in a container. Remember that it mustn't contain any hard lumps. When heating the flour on a low flame, if we don't stop moving it, it won't get hard. You can also heat it in the oven at a low temperature, covered with something so it doesn't burn, and then sieving it. There must never be bones in croquettes. Be very careful. Before mixing the milk and flour, add the chopped onion, etc. to the milk. Pour the boiling milk into the flour and mix it as quickly as possible to get a boiling or scalded dough. You can use a spoon or wooden spatula if there isn't a lot to mix, or a manual or electric whisk if the amount is greater. If mixing manually, you have to do it without stopping to get a good, quick mixture. This will be softer than *churro* dough because it has more fat, but it will still be easy to manage with the hands.

If you are working the dough manually, put some flour on the table so it doesn't stick to the table or your hands. Then form a bar with the dough and cut slices the size of a croquette with a knife. Each slice is rolled under the hands into oval shapes, making sure they are all the same. In a suitable container, such as a frying pan, put a spoonful of beaten egg, enough to just finely layer the pan with moisture. Put the croquettes on top of this and roll them so that they become glazed with the egg while keeping their oval form. Then roll them in breadcrumbs, shave off any loose crumbs and they're ready. You can keep them separately frozen, in groups by using waterproof paper, or in plastic boxes or packages to be used as you need them. Then you can dry them and fry them. Machines to make croquettes can be bought from catering machinery suppliers. Or you can invent one yourself. In these recipes, use common products, good quality and low cost. Frozen croquettes can be served for selling in a catering business or wholesale.

SELLING CROQUETTES WHOLESALE. 330

To sell croquettes wholesale, wrap them in plastic bags with our brand on at a certain weight. When wrapping them frozen, keep them separate from each other. Then as long as you keep them frozen, they won't stick together. These explanations are very simple but explicit enough so that you know how to sell another product wholesale. We've already seen how to chain-freeze and mass-freeze products. After covering them in breadcrumbs, put them in a quick-freezing tunnel, and they will come out wrapped and ready. There are both large and small versions of these tunnels. Don't forget that you can make anything. The most important thing is to know what we want to do. We've talked about home-made manufacture and for selling in pubs. To test this, freeze them as we've discussed and then put them in separate bags with the weight which is most suitable for us, and then seal he bag. To know more about these plastic bags, visit or phone one of the factories that makes them. It's better to go along and they'll show you samples with other brands they've already done. You'll get to see sizes and prices.

CROQUETTES FOR MASS-PRODUCTION. 331.

There are machines to resolve this situation for us. One type of machine you can use is a bakery divider machine in the same way they use pieces of pastry dough, all the same. Put a certain amount of dough in the machine, it flattens it and then uses knives to cut it into equal pieces. This is one way to get slices all exactly the same size, as long as the amount we put in the divider is the same. There is also a roller system which rolls the dough first, and one of the rollers has blades on which cut the dough. You can change the distance between the rollers. The longer this distance, the thick the croquettes come out. This is just one idea. We used to make them by hand in my restaurant. Years ago, sweets with made with rollers. Two parallel rollers is one of the great inventions as they have many applications. Of course, catering machine suppliers will have many new inventions now.

APPLE PIE, OR ANY OTHER FRUIT PIE. 332

They can be made on a steel or aluminium tray, rectangular or round, or in special moulds which can be placed in the oven. The idea is to cut out slices or other portions when ordered by customers in the café. Putting up a sign which says: "100 grams fruit pie, so much money", you can get people to start buying. You should also put up the price per kilo, per slice and per complete pie. If the price needs to be competitive, they'll buy it both to eat it and take out. Apple pie works at any time of the day, even in the morning.

PASTRY BASE FOR FRUIT PIES. 333

Fruit pies are really easy to make. They sell well if the portions are generous and not too expensive. Recipe for the dough: put a kilo of flour on the work counter. Make in a pit in the centre and put inside 500 grams of margarine, 400 grams of icing sugar, a pinch of cinnamon, a pinch of baking soda from bakery suppliers, half a cup of aniseed and three eggs. Mix it all together within the pit until you get a well-mixed, uniform mixture. Then mix it with the rest of the flour, or use a whisk. This doesn't contain any milk or water. Then you put some of that dough on the table, roll it out with a rolling pan until it has a thickness of around three or four millimetres. Pick it up by rolling it around the rolling pin, put it on a greased tin or mould, cutting it to fit with a knife. Put it in the oven, and when half-cooked, take it out. This can also be used for baked pasties.

FILLING AND FINISHING OFF THE APPLE PIE. 334

The base of the pie is already done when taken out, half-cooked. Put on a centimetre of cream all around it which we've already discussed and know how to make. Then, add thin slices of apple or any other raw fruit, which has had the skin and any hard pieces removed. These slices can be placed in a row on the cream, with one slice covering half of the next one, and so on, until the whole pie is covered. Then paint them with beaten eggs, pour on icing sugar, or paint on melted sugar using an appropriate brush. Put it into a hot oven and it will be done quite quickly, leaving a golden top. Take it out when the top is golden without either the top or bottom being burned. Work out the cost of this to know the price you have to sell each portion. You can also wrap slices of this or individual pieces, as with any other pastry and sell them wholesale. The cream should be made with water so it doesn't go off, as well as the appropriate preservatives.

QUICK CUPCAKES. 335

With this same dough, cut out two circles about 3 or 4 millimetres thick using a mould or glass around 8 cm wide. Put some cream, jam or *cabell d'àngel* in the centre of one of them, put some water around the sides with a brush, and put the other on top, pushing it down to stick them together. On top, you can put some beaten egg with a few drops of vinegar. Sprinkle with some icing sugar or raw, diced almond and cook in the oven. In this way, we can make cheap and tasty pastries for breakfast which can be kept for quite a few days. And they can be sold wholesale.

MANUFACTURING TO MAKE PROFITS. 336

This isn't a cooking course or a kitchen, but fifty years in various trades gives you a lot of experience if you know how to spend your time. So here I can give you some ideas so that if you've never worked in this trade before, you can quickly start doing something until you need a specialist. We always have to do whatever is necessary to achieve our objectives since the reason I'm writing this book is to make you some money. A pub or restaurant kitchen always has quiet times which can be used to do everything I've explained. With puff pastry, you can make as many things as you can think of to sell if your business or, if you prefer, wholesale.

PUFF PASTRY.   337

I remember these recipes from my first job working as a baker. I worked in various different trades and learned from every one of them. Put a kilo of flour on the work counter and make a pit in the centre. In this pit, put two-hundred grams of lard (or margarine), two spoonfuls of vinegar, 10 grams of salt and half a litre of water. Mix these ingredients together, then mix with the rest of the flour and make a compact dough which doesn't easily break off. It must be well kneaded and be manageable with the hands, without being hard or soft. It will be like bread dough.
When it's ready, put it on the table and dust it with flour both on top and underneath so that it doesn't stick to the rolling pin or the table. Next we roll it out with the rolling pin, trying to make it rectangular, about twice as long as it is wide, and about half a centimetre thick. Pinch all along the borders to make sure the butter doesn't get out. Add a kilo of lukewarm margarine or lard, or at least, which isn't cold, and spread it out equally over the entire surface of the dough. When the margarine has cooled, fold the dough into three, as if it were a leaflet of three pages. First close the first third towards the centre, and then the other third to cover it. You will end up with three layers and the margarine inside it.
Now, knead the dough again without unfolding it, putting down some more flour for reasons we've talked about, and stretch it out again using the rolling pin. Then fold it into three again. You end up folding the dough four times: once

with margarine and three without. The last time is the final shape you'll keep.

FINISHING THE DOUGH AND MILLEFEUILLE. 338

Cut slices or pieces off the dough to make whichever pastries you want. To make millefeuille, take a slice of dough, small or medium-sized, and roll it out until it is around two or thre millimetres thick. Then place it on a baking tray using the rolling pin. The rectangular tray should be completely covered by the dough. Cut off any overhanging dough. Before placing in the oven, prick the dough with a fork or spatula so it doesn't shrink. The overhanging pieces you cut off can be used to make another, adding a little of the original dough. You should make three exactly the same. When they are cooked and have cooled again, put one of the three on a display tray used to show in your pub or café. Fill it with a layer of cream and put on top a layer of meringue, a centimetre thick, dust on some cinnamon and put another layer of puff pastry. Then layer again with cream, meringue and a final third puff pastry layer, and it is done. Take a serrated knife and dip the blade in water so it cuts cleanly. Cut off the sides to leave it completely uniform. Make every cut downwards, like any cake, as if you were cutting wood, and not crushing the cake downwards too. Cut into whatever pieces you want. Dust with icing sugar and cinnamon and take them to the counter.

Note: When we are making the puff pastry dough, when folding the layers onto each other, if the joins at the sides are not perfect, the pieces you cut will end up twisted, and the highest part will fall to one side. When the dough is finished, it's better to remove around half a centimetre all around it with a hot knife before you start using it.

PASTRIES. 339

This puff pastry dough can also be used to make pastries and pies such as you see in many places. It's best to copy the shapes and types that you see. If you cut slices about a centimetre thick, ten long and five wide, paint them with beaten egg and put them in the oven, you can make many things. For example, you can make pasties and other types of pies. Millefeuille can be made with left-over dough after making other pastries. Make a single mass of dough from these leftovers together in your hands, and roll it out with a rolling pin. Make sure to prick it well before placing in the oven otherwise it may shrink.

ANOTHER RECIPE: ELEPHANT EARS (PALMIERS). 340

Roll out some dough until it is more or less rectangular, about three millimetres thick. Dust it with icing sugar all over both sides so it doesn't stick to the table or the rolling pin. Starting at one side, fold about two or three centimetres towards the centre, then fold again over itself and continue folding until you reach the centre. Then do the same starting at the opposite side.

NEXT, JOIN ONE OF THE FOLDED FACES TOGETHER WITH THE OTHER. 341

Now we should have a more or less rectangular bar of dough. With a hot or serrated knife, cut slices around three, four or more centimetres thick, making sure not to crush when cutting down. Turn over these slices over so that the cut is face down on the table and the widest part facing upwards. (This is looking over the grain of the folds.) With the palm of your hand near to the thumb, crush down the down until you get the form of the palmier, putting on a little more icing sugar to make sure it doesn't stick to the table or your hand. Dampen a cloth with oil and wipe it on the trays you're going to use to bake the dough so it doesn't stick. You can put beaten egg on the upper part of the dough, as long as it isn't made with coconut or chocolate. Then you bake them in the oven.

COCONUT AND CHOCOLATE PALMIERS. 342

They are made exactly the same as before but without the beaten egg. You then coat them in chocolate as we've discussed earlier. Coat one side first using a brush if you like, and when it is dry, coat the other side. Coconut Palmiers are made by painting one side lightly with syrup and then putting on grains of coconut. Many bakery businesses now exist which manufacture this as well as sponge cake, biscuits and pastries, wrap them small transparent individual bags, and they are doing very well. To be a good business, you really need a professional cook. But knowing these recipes, you won't be a total novice.

WRAPPING AND SEALING MACHINES. 343

These machines are extremely simple. The pastries go in one side and so does the paper. The machine wraps, seals and cuts the package for you. As easy as that. Where can you find these types of machines? Simple: look in the Valencia telephone directory (for Spain) or whatever country you're in and look for the address... Or ask for information in your city's Chamber of Commerce. Ask when the Bakery Machinery exhibition is being held. They'll have other machines for any other product you want to manufacture or handle at the appropriate exhibitions. You'll be surprised when you see how many machines there are available to see. These exhibitions take place in all countries. You can also find out in the Chambers of Commerce where this machinery is sold.

BRANDS AND PATENTS. 344

Photocopies of any recipe for a product, such as chocolate powder, soups, flans, bags of frozen food, other food, or any other product which is registered, can be obtained from the appropriate official registry through the brands and patents registration companies by paying a little money. All you need to do is take to the appropriate company a packet of the product you want information about. This is legal and make it possible for you to know which products are registered, for how long, and its recipe. You'll get photocopies of the declaration from the person or society that patented or registered it and a list of the ingredients it contains, so you'll know what you can and can't do. You can't copy a recipe exactly or the brand name, but you can make your own version with your name, brand and recipe which can be similar in proportions but not exactly the same. You can make any other product with the same objective as long as the recipe is similar, but not exactly the same. Chocolate, soup, flan or anything else which doesn't look like anything else being sold should be perfectly legal.

OTHER EXAMPLES OF PRODUCTS FOR WHOLESALE. 345

Rice, chickpeas, beans, flour, *gofio* from the Canary Islands, packet soups, flan and many other products which can be wrapped up can be marketed, as well as any others you come up with. Even packet has its seal, brand and wrapper. There is a lot of money to be made in vegetables, since it's easy and cheap to buy the ingredients, wrap them in small quantities, once prepared, and sell them wholesale to shops, retailers and distribution warehouses. In order to package vegetables well, there is a very good book which explains it to you. I've got an orchard and, in order for the dried broad beans to work as seeds for the next year, I put them in a closed flask and put a clove of garlic inside. I'm not saying you should use garlic for all of your vegetables, but there is probably some liquid you can spray on them to make sure they don't rot. Look for preservatives for wholesalers who sell chemical products for food. All of these explanations about packaging refer to this, packaging for food. It's very difficult for other products to be packaged and sold in the same way. Anything is possible though. It's useful to have the tap water to make the drink in the back of the shop in a fridge or ice-making machine which gives us as much as we ant.

You will have seen in some businesses those machines which spray out cold water when you press the tab which you can drink. I think they must be connected to the water mains. I used to have a bar of ice in the fridge and used that to cool the water I used to make the frozen drinks. When we made the drinks, it was good to put the sugar in some water at room temperature, then add the syrup, and once it was mixed, add the very cold water and keep it all in the fridge as needed. I didn't even need to put it in the fridge since the sales were so constant. This was my invention for making really cold iced drinks.

That's what customers want. And I told myself, you want it cold, you can have it cold, and I sold drinks continuously on every summer day. They were small premises but located on the high street of a neighbourhood with around fifty thousand inhabitants. I'm bombarding you with ideas here and repeating them so you remember them. This is how you learn, by repeating what you read. Customers have to notice that the drinks have a good taste and at a good price, as well as being cold. The cups can be plastic so that people get used to walking in the street with our drinks, advertising for us. I used to sell them in glasses though, and they drank them inside. They were quarter of a litre, and I sold them at half of the price of any cola or lemon drink of any big brand.

THE SECRET TO SELLING A LOT. 346

The secret to selling a lot isn't just in the price or the taste, even though there was plenty of sugar. The majority of people like it because it was quick service, a really intense cold in which flakes of ice floated in the drinks, not like those shavings which seem like candy floss, and because of the good, personal customer service. They couldn't ask for much more anyway since the premises was only 26 m2. But the location was in the centre of a busy area. As you see, a business which isn't big is better than a business which doesn't sell.

BUYING THE PRODUCT. 347

The region of Valencia in Spain in the biggest producer of citrus syrup and tiger nut *horchata* in Spain. This region and oranges are inseparable. This produce is sold by the syrup factories in this region, and you can buy orange, lemon and tiger nut *horchata* as the most traditional syrups. The addresses of these businesses can be found in the Yellow Pages (under syrup manufacturers) and may have representatives in your city. If you're in another country, ask food wholesalers in your area who can tell you where to buy the product from or sell it to you themselves.

PREPARING THE DRINK. 348

I'll tell you how to make it. In a new ten-litre bucket, put three litres of concentrated syrup, whether orange or lemon, and half a kilo of sugar. If it isn't very sweet, add a little more sugar and mix it well in the water. Finish by filling the bucket with cold water. It is ready to be frozen now. Some customers are very clever and will want it to be made with all natural orange or lemon juice at a very good price, but this isn't possible. They are the minority, and since we're aiming for a majority, we're fine as we are.
This recipe is enough to get a good product as long as it is accompanied by low temperatures. *Horchata* can made in the same bucket, with a litre of concentrated syrup and 500 grams of sugar. The taste and sweetness have to be controlled when making it for the first time. Don't let anyone tell you to put in more syrup, because you wouldn't be competitive. Overnight, leave the three parts of the container completely full. There should be at least 20 to 25 litres of each *horchata*, orange and lemon, as an example. Make it at the proportions you decide. In relation to the chest freezer, it should be made of acid-proof stainless steel or anodised aluminium. This will avoid it being damaged by the liquid passing through the coils to cool the drinks.

SELLING THE PRODUCT. 349

As I've been saying throughout the book, it's essential that the location of the business be in a place where many people walk past, such as in a busy commercial area of a busy area of a city. The first day, or the first few days, you can give away small glasses for lemonade for free. It doesn't matter if you don't make any money, even though that's what you will think at first. That direct publicity will get you many more customers. Sales will come at the same time you invite people to taste your drinks. Every person that receives something for free will leave them with a little reminder, and they'll remember you every time they walk past your business. Do you know why? Because we lived in a world with so much selfishness that when we get something for free, it almost seems normal.

Put a sign outside with a price for cup and per litre to take away. Remember not to set the prices too high because you'll never sell much and every day you'll sell more. The best weapon in this battle is to give people something for free, even if they don't buy anything else. Did you know that drug dealers give people their first drugs for free until they are addicted? Then they sell plenty. You have to do the same with your iced drinks. When we tried selling these drinks, if customers asked for a bottled drink, we'd try to sell them ours which was unsuccessful. After thinking about it well (thinking is very important), when they asked for a bottled drink, we'd give them what they wanted. Then we would get them half a cup of our drink saying it was on the house. The bottled drink was cold from the fridge, but ours was super-cold, with flakes of ice floating in it. The next day, or a few days later, those customers came back to our business and asked us for the drink we'd given them to try. Infallible publicity which worked well.

Many people will say "Bloody hell! It's so cold!" But then after they've finished it, they'll say "Give me a lemon one this time". We had orange, lemon and tiger nut *horchata*, and that was enough. Some customers would get throat infections or tonsillitis. Maybe they didn't have the natural defences to cope, or they drank them too quickly, who knows. I remember one woman who came with her son and asked me "Do you know this boy? He's my son." She said, "Please, if my son comes in and drinks a lemonade, don't sell him another one because he comes home with a sore throat." If you live in a place with a hot climate, you'll sell a lot more iced drinks every day. The method you use to get these low temperatures should be kept secret. Your competitors won't know how you do it and think that people don't drink iced drinks any more, while you sell more every day.Clarification: When I tell you my business secrets here, I want my readers to understand how they can achieve whatever they want by working and creating work and products which can be sold.

QUALITY CATERING MACHINERY. 350

Websites where you can find businesses, products and services in the catering trade on a national level. In Spain www.nan.es You can also find good-quality catering machinery in SAMMIC.- Organisation and sales,- Atxubiaga Street, 14- .-20730 Azpeitia (Guipúzcoa) Tel: 943 157095,- Fax,: 943 150190. ventas@sammic.com

Thank you, my friends, for having read this far. If you have understood everything I've written, you are ready to enter the world of businesses with the assurance you won't fail.

LIST OF SANDWICHES. 351

SNACK SALES MADE IN THE ACT					
HAMBURGER TOMATO	GRILLED BEEF STEAK	GRILLED PORK LETTUCE TOMATO	CHICKEN BREAT GRILL WITH MAYONNEISE	FRIED CHICKEN MAYONNEISE AND TOMATO
N° 1 ___ €	N° 2 2.50 €	N° 3 ___ €	N° 4 ___ €	N° 5 ___ €
TUNA MAYONNEISE AND TOMATO	HAM CHEESE AND TOMATO	SARDINES IN OIL AND FRIED PEPPER	CHORIZO FRIED WITH PEPPERS	MANCHEGO CHEESE AND TOMATO
N° 6 ___ €	N° 7 ___ €	N° 8 ___ €	N° 9 ___ €	N° 10 ___ €
OMELETTE AND PEPPERS	ONION OMELETTE	HAM GHERKINS PICKLED SAUSAGE	FRIED SQUIN AND MAYONNEISE	AND GHERKINS PICKLED SAUSAGE
N° 11 ___ €	N° 12 ___ €	N° 13 ___ €	N° 14 ___ €	N° 15 ___ €
PIPPER BACON AND MAYONNEISE	SERRANO HAM TOMATO IOL	HAM SHRIMP TOMATO TORTILLA	ASPARAGUS OMEMETTE MAYONNEISE	TUNA TORTILLA MAYONAISE
N° 16 ___ €	N° 17 ___ €	N° 18 ___ €	N° 19 ___ €	N° 20 ___ €
BOLOGNA CHEESE LETUCCE	SOBRASADA CHEESE LETTUCE	HARD-BOILED EGGS AND MAYONEISE	BREADED PORK LOIN AND MAYONENIESE	FRIED PRAWNS MAYONNAISE
N° 21 ___ €	N° 22 ___ €	N° 23 ___ €	N° 24 ___ €	N° 25 ___ €
SERVING CROQUETTES	PORTION OF MEATBALLS	PORTION OF SALAD	SALAD LETUTCE AND TOMATO	SERVING FRIES CALAMARI
N° 26 ___ €	N° 27 ___ €	N° 28 ___ €	N° 29 ___ €	N° 30 ___ €
PORTION OF GARLIC PRAWNS	CALAMARI	PORTION OF ANCHOVIES	PORTION OF GRILLED PRAWNS	PORTION OF SPICY POTATOES
N° 31 ___ $€	N° 32 ___ $	N° 33 ___ $	N° 34 ___ $	N° 35 ___ $
Road chicker takeaway	Serves several takeaway			To paella rice togo

Synopsis, Author **Rafael López Gómez.** 1

INTRODUCTION - 2
CHAPTER 1 - -3

BEGINNING AS A BUSINESS-PERSON 3
WORKING FOR YOURSELF OR FOR OTHERS. 4
ALWAYS FORWARDS. 5
WORKING AS AN EMPLOYEE AND HAVING NO RESPONSIBILITIES. 6
INGENUITY HELPS US. 7
DOWHATEVER YOU'REDOING 8
BEING WIDE AWAKE WHEN YOU'RE NOT ASLEEP.9 INITIAL CAPITAL. 10
GET USED TO THINKING. 11
BRAND MARKET, WEAKER ECONOMY 12
MY PROPOSAL, IF YOU HAVE NOTHING. 13
EXTRA JOBS, A GOOD SOURCE OF INCOME.14
WORKING AT WEEKENDS. 15
FAST-FOOD COMPANIES. 16
SEARCHING FOR MORE INTERESTING WORK 17
ANOTHER OF FINDING THESE JOBS. 18
WHAT YOU CAN EARN AS A WAITER - IN

BANQUETS. 19
RESTAURANTS THAT SPECIALISE IN BANQUETS 20
WORKING EXTRA TO INCREASE YOUR INCOME. 21
MAY YOUR IDEAS PREVAIL. 22
STARTING A BUSINESS   23
WHAT IS BEHIND WHAT CONSUME?   24
TEAMWORK.   25
SPONSORS.   26
HAVING EMPLOYEES THROUGH NECESSITY. 27
SECURITY IN THE RUNNING OF THE BUSINESS.28
FIGHT AND WORK FOR YOUR FUTURE. 29
SUCCESS FOLLOWS THE ASTUTE AND THE SHREWD.30
YOUR KNOWLEDGE WILL HELP YOU SUCCEED.31
CALLING LUCK.   32
STARTING YOUR FIRST BUSINESS   33
DO WHATEVER WILL GET PEOPLE IN YOUR PREMISES. 34
DON'T SCRIMP ON PUBLICITY.   35
KNOW WHAT OTHERS ARE DOING   36
ISPONSORS. 37

INTERNAL MOVEMENT. 38

YOU NEVER KNOW HOW FAR YOU CAN GET. 39

LIMITATION OF COMMAND. 40

THE MANAGER AND THEIR MISSION. 40.A

THE COMPLETE POWER OF THE COMPANY 41

INFLUENCES AND THEIR EFFECTS. 42

ADVERTISING. 43

RHYTHM FROM THE FIRST DAY. 44

ON EXPENSES AND STOCK. 45

PAYING EMPLOYEES WITH PROFITS. 46

GENERALISING INCENTIVES NEVER GIVES GOOD RESULTS. 47

PREVIOUS JOBS, 48

CHAPTER 2 49

OPENING A PUB. 50

LET'S START WITH THE BARS. 51

THE WALLS OF THE PUB. 52

GENTS TOILETS. 53

LADIES TOILETS. 54

TOILETS AND CUSTOMERS. 55

TOILETS AND CHANGING ROOMS FOR EMPLOYEES. 56

STOREROOM FOR STOCK. 57

MINIMUM EQUIPMENT REQUIRED IN THE KITCHEN OF THE PUB. 58-------BUSINESS. 59

A COLLABORATOR TO HELP START THE

THE TILL. 60

SELLING SANDWICHES. 61

SANDWICH SIGN. 62

(SANDWICH SIGN EXAMPLE ON NEXT PAGE) 63

FROZEN BREAD ROLLS. 64

SANGRIA AND AN INVITATION. 65

MINI CANAPÉS AND LOW COST TAPAS. 66

PUBS WITH FOOD IN TOURIST AREAS. 67

GIVING AWAY SOMETHING FOR FREE ALWAYS GIVES GOOD RESULTS. 68

THE WEEKLY DAY OF REST. 69

DIFFERENT TYPES OF CATERING BUSINESSES. 70

TAPAS PUBS. 71

SANDWICH SHOPS IN TOURIST AREAS. 72

WAITERS IN TOURIST AREAS. 73

PUBS WITH REGULARS. 74

LOCAL PUBS. 75

TABLES IN OTHER PUBS. 76

THE CAFÉ TRADITION. 77

PUBS IN COMMERCIAL AREAS OF CITIES. 78
LUNCHTIME SERVICE. 79
PROFITS THROUGH FOOD. 80
THE COST OF A POPULAR MENU. 81
STARTING A BUSINESS OF DIRECT SALE TO THE PUBLIC. 82
CAN I OPEN A BUSINESS SELLING GLASSES OF WINE? 83
METHODS FOR GETTING CUSTOMERS. 84
OTHER GOOD THINGS TO SELL A PUB. 85
YOUR STAFF'S GOOD CUSTOMER SERVICE. 86
GENERALISING INCENTIVES NEVER GIVES GOOD RESULTS.   87
PREVIOUS JOBS, 88
OPENING A CAFÉ 90

CHAPTER 3---   89

UPPER-CLASS CATERING BUSINESSES. 91
OPENING A NORMAL CAFÉ.   92
WHEN WILL IT START MAKING ME MONEY? 93
POPULAR CAFÉ . 94
TRADES WHICH ARE NEW TO YOU. 95

GENERAL LAYOUT. 96
EXAMPLE OF THE LAYOUT OF PREMISES WITH A SIZE OF 200 M2. 97
SSENTIALS. 98
THE BAR OR COUNTER. 99
SIZE OF THE BAR. 100
DISPLAY WINDOWS IN THE BAR. 101
WHY DON'T SOME BUSINESSES HAVE DISPLAY WINDOWS? 102
DISHWASHER AT THE BAR. 103
DRAUGHT BEER. 104
INSTALLING A BEER ON TAP. 105
THE COFFEE MACHINE. 106
CONSUMPTION OF COFFEE. 107
COFFEE GRINDER. 108
IMPORTANT COFFEE MACHINES. 109
OPENING A CAFÉ IN THE MORNING. 110
STAFF WORKING HOURS. 111
POPULAR CAFÉ. 112
COMBINATION PLATTERS AND OTHER MEALS. 113
IDEAS FOR A COMBINATION PLATTER. 114
DESSERT AND COFFEE MENU. 115

PHOTOS OF COMBINED PLATTERS. 116

TAKING THE ORDER. 117

COST AND SALE PRICES ON COMBINATION PLATTERS. 118

BREAD, DRINKS AND DESSERTS. 119

KITCHENS IN CAFÉS. 120

KITCHEN EQUIPMENT. 121

VENTILATION FOR YOUR PREMISES. 122

THE GRILL. 123

MICROWAVE OVEN. 124

ICED DRINKS MACHINES IN VIEW OF THE PUBLIC. 125

AMOUNT OF COFFEE NEEDED FOR ICED COFFEE. 126

VARIOUS FLAVOURS OF SYRUP FOR USE IN ICED DRINKS. 127

THINKING LIKE A FACTORY IS VERY GOOD FOR BUSINESS. 128

ICE-CREAMS. 129

COMPETING USING ICE-CREAMS. 130

THE TILL. 131

SPIRITS. 132

SPARE GLASSES AND BOTTLES. 133

GAMIN GENTERTAINMENT MACHINES. 134

SELLING TOBACCO. 135

GENERAL STORAGE. 136

CONTROL OFFICE. 137

TOAST. 138

HOW TO SELL A LOT OF "HOUSE TOAST". 139

ORIGINAL CAFÉ. 140

HOW TO SELL A LOT OF COFFEE. 141

BREAD AND PASTRIES. 142

CLOSING TIME. 143

END OF THE DAY, CLEANING AND RESTOCKING. 144

THE TILL. 145

TAPAS AT THE END OF THE EVENING. 146

IMPORTANCE OF WEARING UNIFORMS. 147

THE IMPORTANT THING ABOUT CAFÉS. 148

MISTAKES IN THE ORDERS. 149

OTHER ITEMS TO TAKE AWAY. 150

CHAPTER 4   151

RESTAURANTS WITH TAKE-AWAY FOOD   152
PREMISES AND LOCATION. 153
LAYOUT OF THE PREMISES. 154
ESSENTIAL EQUIPMENT FOR TAKE-AWAY RESTAURANTS. 155
PRODUCTS AND SELLING TO THE PUBLIC. 156
KITCHEN FOR THESE SPECIALITIES. 157
FOCUS OF THE BUSINESS. 158
HOW CUSTOMERS ACT. 159
WHAT THE CUSTOMER SEES WHILE BEING SERVED. 160
THE STAFF'S ABILITIES. 161
MANAGING THIS BUSINESS. 162
TRADITIONAL MEALS FROM THAT AREA. 163
PACKAGES FOR FOOD. 164
SALES AND WORK HOURS. 165
STUDY, OFFICE AND SO ON. 166
OPENING DAY. 167
THE VITAL MOMENT OF THE CUSTOMERS' VISIT. 168
PUBLICITY AND SELLERS. 169

TRADE NAME. 170

EAT-IN RESTAURANTS. 171

ONE SWALLOW DOESN'T MAKE A SUMMER, BUT IT'LL HELP YOU OUT. 172

ROTISSERIE FOR CHICKENS ON VIEW. 173

SPECIAL TRAYS FOR FREEZING. 174

CHAPTER 5 - 175

SELF-SERVICE RESTAURANT OR CAFÉ 176

SELF-SERVICE, A SIMPLE SPECIALITY. 177

ADVERTISING. 178

TYPE OF FOOD SERVED. 180

GENERAL SUPERVISOR. 181

WORKING-CLASS CONSUMERS. 182

CUSTOMER ENTERS THE RESTAURANT. 183

DISPLAY COUNTER. 184

SHELF TO PLACE TRAYS ON. 185

.FOOD COLLECTION PASSAGE. 186

COLD MEALS AND HORS D'OEUVRES. 187

FIRST COURSES. 188

SECOND COURSES. 189

CHILDREN'S MENU. 190

THE DESSERTS ARE NEXT. 191
AND THEN THE DRINKS. 192
FILL IT WITH ICE CUBES UP TO THE TOP!"
(AND THE PRICE). ICE CUBES. 193
STAFF IN CHARGE OF RESTOCKING. 194

VISIBLE PRICES. 195
COST EXAMPLES.. 196
CUSTOMER SERVICE. 197
SUCCESS DEPENDS ON INTELLIGENCE. 198
THE PREMISES WILL ALWAYS END UP BEING SMALL. 199
FIXTURES. 200
MORE TABLES, OPPORTUNITY FOR MORE SALES. 201
IF CUSTOMERS ORDER COFFEE. 202
WAITERS AND TIPS. 203
SHARINGOUT COMMISSION. 204
THE RELATIONSHIP BETWEEN TABLES AND TRAYS. 205
CONNECTION BETWEEN COUNTER AND KITCHEN. 206
DINING ROOM CHAIRS AND TABLES. 207

SIZE OF THE PREMISES. 208
VENTILATION. 209
PUBLIC AND STAFF TO
ILETS. 210
DAYS OFF IN CATERING. 211
THE OTHER TYPE OF LUCK: GAMBLING. 212
DISHES AND CUTLERY. 213
THE KITCHEN. 214
SELF-SERVICE CAFÉS. 215
CHAPTER 6 - 216
RESTAURANTS FOR BANQUETS, WEDDINGS, COMMUNIONS AND SO ON. 217
LARGE-SCALE BANQUETS. 218
EXAMPLE OF ECONOMIC CALCULATIONS DURING BANQUETS. 219
CUSTOMER OPPORTUNITIES. 220
CUSTOMERS VISITING LOOKING FOR A FREE DAY TO - HAVE A BANQUET. 221
PAYING FOR THE BANQUET. 222
THE MEANS OF PAYMENT. 223
THE DISCO. 224
EXAMPLE OF A WEDDING MEAL. 225
ABOUT MUSIC AND DANCING AT THE

BANQUET. 226

TOILETS AT BANQUETS. 227

THE KITCHEN FOR BANQUETS. 228

THE KITCHEN HAS TO WORK LIKE A FACTORY. 229

THE SAME WAITERS FOR THE SAME BANQUETS. 230

DESSERTS CHAMPAGNE OR CAVA. 231

COFFEE SERVICE. 232

PERMANENT EMPLOYEES. 233

BUILDING AND DINING TABLES. 234

MULTIPLE TABLES. 235

VENTILATION. 236

STAFF UNIFORM. 237

.OTHER RECOMMENDATIONS. 238

PLACES WHERE THESE BUSINESS WORK WELL. 239

ABOUT RENTING OR BUYING AN INDUSTRIAL PREMISES. 240

MENUS FOR BANQUETS WHEN "STARTING OUT" 241

COST CALCULATIONS. 242

FOOD STORAGE. 243

THE NEED FOR PUBLICITY. 244

CHAPTER 7   245

ALL-YOU-CAN-EAT BUFFETS.   246
HOW THE BUSINESS WORKS.   247
DRINKS. 248
SUITABLE FURNITURE.   249
CUSTOMERS AT AN ALL-YOU-CAN-EAT BUFFET. 250
WHERE TO SET UP THIS TYPE OF BUSINESS. 251
DELIVERING FOOD TO HOMES OR UNDER CONTRACT TO OTHER CUSTOMERS. 252
WHEN SHOULD I GIVE THEM THE BILL TO PAY? 253
CATERING SERVICE TO BUSINESSES. 254
CATERING SERVICE TO SCHOOLS. 255
THE DELIVERY VAN. 256
THE KITCHEN.   257
STOREROOM.   258
KITCHEN STAFF.   259
ECONOMIC CALCULATIONS. 260
LOCATION FOR A CATERING BUSINESS. 261

OTHER PRODUCTS MADE IN CATERING BUSINESSES.- 262
HOT CHOCOLATE WITH *CHURROS* AND THEIR TRADITIONS. 263
INSTALLING THESE MACHINES. 264
CHURRO FRYING PANS. 265
RECIPE FOR THIN *CHURRO* DOUGH, MADE MANUALLY. 266
PREPARING "*CHURROS*" 267
MIXER. 268
ELECTRICAL MACHINES USED FOR MAKING *CHURROS*. 269
PRICES AND METHODS OF SELLING. 270
CHURROS SOLD IN CORNER SHOPS AND ON THE MOVE. 271
SELLING *CHURROS* AT FAIRS. 272
FROZEN *CHURROS* FOR SELLING WHOLESALE. 273
MANUFACTURING THICK, SOFT *CHURROS*. 274
FRITTERS. 275
PREPARING FRITTERS. 276
FRIED FLAT CAKES. 277
BERLINERS (ANOTHER TYPE OF DOUGHNUT). 278

CREAM FOR FILLING DOUGHNUTS AND SO ON. 279

CHOCOLATE-FLAVOURED CREAM. 280

VEGETABLE FOOD COLOURING. 281

EXAMPLES OF COLOURING AND ESSENCES. 282

SLICED POTATOES. 283

PRE-COOKED FROZEN POTATOES. 284

INDUSTRIAL PROCESS FOR FROZEN POTATOES. 285

FREEZING EN MASSE. 286

WINE *PESTIÑOS*. 287

FORMING THE *PESTIÑOS*. 288

FINISHING OFF THE *PESTIÑOS*. 289

ANOTHER COATING FOR *PESTIÑOS*. 290

CLARIFICATION ON THE POINT OF USING SUGAR WHEN BOILING. 291

PASTY DOUGH. 292

SWEET PASTIES. 293

SAVOURY PASTIES. 294

INEXPENSIVE JAMS. 295

CABELL D'ÀNGEL ("ANGEL HAIR") 296

CRYSTALLISED FRUITS. 297

FRUIT COATED IN CHOCOLATE. 298

CHAPTER 8   299

CAFÉS SELLING HOT CHOCOLATE, *CHURROS*, GRILLED CHICKEN, LEMONADE AND SO ON. 300
GRILLED CHICKEN. 301
SELL WHAT WE MAKE OURSELVES. 302
SETTING UP THE BUSINESS AND HOW IT WORKS. 303
PACKAGING FOR TAKE-AWAY FOOD. 304
OTHER USEFUL ITEMS FOR THE DINING ROOM. 305
EXTRACTOR FAN IN THE KITCHEN. 306
TAKE-AWAY COUNTER. 307
TABLES FOR EATING IN. 308
CLASS OF RESTAURANT. 309
MANAGING A BUSINESS IS AN ART WHICH IS LEARNED. 310
ADVERTISING. 311
IMITATING ANTS. 312
SIGNS WHICH SELL. 313
ABOUT HOT CHOCOLATE. 314
MAKE YOUR OWN CHOCOLATE. 315
DEFINITIVE TESTS WITH THE CHOCOLATE. 316

HAVING HOT CHOCOLATE IN A FLASK READY TO SERVE. 317

CRUNCHY, RECENTLY-MADE *CHURROS*. 318

MORE ABOUT GRILLED CHICKENS. 319

ABOUT SELLING A LOT OF TOAST. 320

FRENCH TOAST WITH MILK. 321

FRENCH TOAST WITH WINE. 322

SECOND BUSINESS: COPY THE FIRST ONE. 323

CHAPTER 9-- 324

DIFFERENT PRODUCTS FOR SELLING WHOLESALE OR DIRECTLY TO CUSTOMERS.

HOT HOCOLATE POWDER. 325

HOT CHOCOLATE POWDER FOR SELLING. 371

WHOLESALE. 326

PUBS AND CAFÉS. 327

MARKETING INSTANT HOT CHOCOLATE FOR MANUFACTURE OF CROQUETTES. 328

METHOD OF PREPARATION FOR CROQUETTES. 329

SELLING CROQUETTES WHOLESALE. 330

CROQUETTES FOR MASS-PRODUCTION. 331.

APPLE PIE, OR ANY OTHER FRUIT PIE. 332
PASTRY BASE FOR FRUIT PIES. 333
FILLING AND FINISHING OFF THE APPLE PIE. 334
QUICK CUPCAKES. 335
MANUFACTURING TO MAKE PROFITS. 336
PUFF PASTRY. 337
FINISHING THE DOUGH AND MILLEFEUILLE. 338
PASTRIES. 339
ANOTHER RECIPE: ELEPHANT EARS (PALMIERS). 340
NEXT, JOIN ONE OF THE FOLDED FACES TOGETHER WITH THE OTHER. 341
COCONUT AND CHOCOLATE PALMIERS. 342
WRAPPING AND SEALING MACHINES. 343
BRANDS AND PATENTS. 344
OTHER EXAMPLES OF PRODUCTS FOR WHOLESALE. 345
THE SECRET TO SELLING A LOT. 346
BUYING THE PRODUCT. 347
PREPARING THE DRINK. 348
SELLING THE PRODUCT. 349
QUALITY CATERING MACHINERY. 350
LIST OF SANDWICHES..351

WHY DO SOME ENTREPRENEURS SUCCEED OR FAIL? **J. Rafael López**

WHY DO SOME ENTREPRENEURS SUCCEED OR FAIL? J. Rafael López

WHY DO SOME ENTREPRENEURS SUCCEED OR FAIL? **J. Rafael López**

WHY DO SOME ENTREPRENEURS SUCCEED OR FAIL? J. Rafael López

www.ingramcontent.com/pod-product-compliance
Lightning Source LLC
Chambersburg PA
CBHW051632170526

45167CB00001B/154